Use your brain to beat
A D D I C T I O N

Use your brain to beat
A D D I C T I O N

the complete guide
to understanding and tackling addiction

SUSAN ALDRIDGE
SERIES EDITOR **RITA CARTER**

First published in Great Britain in 2005 by Cassell Illustrated,
a division of Octopus Publishing Group Ltd.,
2–4 Heron Quays, London, E14 4JP

ISBN: 1-84403-135-7
EAN: 9781844031351

Editor: Joanne Wilson
Design: DW Design
Index: Indexing Specialists (UK) Ltd

Contents

Introduction

Addiction is a world-wide condition which creates problems for an estimated 5 per cent of the world's adult population.* Many addictive substances are physically dangerous. For instance, recent research confirms that persistent smokers die younger and can expect to lose, on average, ten years of life because of their habit. And dependence on drugs which are outlawed, like heroin and cocaine, is inevitably damaging because users are often forced into criminality, with all its attendant social risks. Why do people take such risks with their lives? This book examines the "need" to take drugs – addiction – to feel pleasure, relaxation, or just to be able to function, in face of all the risks and the dangers misuse brings.

In Part One: Understanding addiction, we explore the roots of addiction in our physical make-up, with special reference to the role played by the brain and nervous system, and our genes. The most common types of addiction: smoking, alcohol misuse, self-damaging behaviours, like compulsive gambling and shopping, and illegal drug use, are each considered separately, along with the wide range of up-to-date treatments. We show how drug molecules act on the pleasure circuits and reward centres of the brain, creating dependences through changes in gene activity that actually "remodel" the brain – altering the relationship between the individual and their drug or behaviour of choice. The latest brain research reveals the common pathways of addiction and why addiction to, say, gambling, can be as hard to erase as an addiction to heroin.

* United Nations Office on Drugs and Crime, World Drug Report, 2004.

This section also points out the problems of defining and recognising addiction and considers its effect both on the individual, and on society as a whole. We aim to give a clear description of the science of addiction and to demystify a condition which is often treated as a moral failure or a sign of weak character rather than a brain disease to which each and every one of us is vulnerable.

Is there hope for the addict? Yes, certainly, for in Part Two we provide well-researched and scientifically accurate evidence for the efficacy of treatments for the more common addictions. For instance, nicotine replacment and/or bupropion work for many smokers wanting to quit. We also look at new drugs for treating alcohol misuse as well as the well established treatment for opiate misuse, methadone, and some more recent advances in this area. But medical treatment alone is rarely enough to produce sustained recovery from addiction. Psychological treatments and support play an invaluable role. We look at some of these approaches, such as cognitive behaviour therapy and recently researched intervention therapy (based on the contact that is found between health-care professionals and sufferers of addiction), and how they can be effective. Beating an addiction is truly a tough challenge – whether it's smoking, heroin, gambling or some other compulsive and destructive behaviour. This book shows how a better understanding of how addiction affects the brain is the key to understanding and recovery.

Part One
Understanding addiction

1 Addiction today

"Our society makes artificial distinctions among addictive drugs, fostering the false impression that because nicotine and alcohol are legal, they must somehow be less dangerous and less addictive than illicit drugs."

Dr Avram Goldstein (Stanford University), *Addiction: From Biology to Drug Policy*, **Oxford University Press, 2001**

What is addiction?

People have always experimented with drugs – out of curiosity, to relax, to have access to spiritual and creative experiences, or just for fun. Similarly, certain *activities* can also exert a similar attraction – sex, gambling, shopping, and even (believe it or not) work. What all these pursuits have in common is that they give us pleasure, by acting on the brain in a way that we are beginning to understand.

When the pursuit of these pleasures gets in the way of everyday tasks and responsibilities, in other words, when they get out of control, we call it dependence, or even addiction. But the problem of addiction is hard to define. As we'll see, smokers are killed by substances in tobacco other than the addictive substance, nicotine. Addicts can, quite often, live a stable life while being addicted. Our perception of the addiction problem depends very much on the drug that's involved. Some addictive substances and behaviours may be benign in their own right, but associated factors (liver damage in alcoholics, for example) do incredible harm.

In this book, we look at addiction as a problem that can be best understood by examining the chemical processes in the brain – although cultural and environmental factors play a huge role. As a result, we look to the brain and the role it plays in governing behaviours to resolve the various problems of addiction. People can, and do, recover from addiction, either on their own or with the help of medical or psychological therapy, or a combination.

What are the characteristic features of addiction?

In its clinical definition, the term addiction is a dependence on a substance (such as alcohol) or an activity (such as gambling) even when the behaviour has become counter-productive to the health of the individual. The individual may not be aware that they are at risk, and it may take a person close to them to notice when this happens. Drinking a bottle of whisky a day or stealing to fund a drug habit are behaviour patterns strongly suggestive of an addiction, but there are also more subtle warning signs. Although addiction can be considered an illness, it can't be diagnosed in the same manner as a purely physical disease such as cancer. Addiction does, however, have certain characteristic features:

■ The addicted individual becomes dependent on a particular substance, behaviour or activity, for the equilibrium of their body and mind.

■ The absence of the substance or behaviour produces a state of physical and/or mental discomfort known as withdrawal.

■ An addict experiences powerful cravings, which may compel them to take self-destructive and/or antisocial measures to obtain their "fix".

■ Addiction is marked by a tolerance. In the case of drugs, this means the addict needs increasing amounts to get the same feeling of comfort or "hit" from it; in the case of alcohol, two or three glasses of wine becomes a whole bottle.

■ Addictive behaviour comes to dominate the individual's life. This can lead to a variety of secondary consequences. For example, a person who continues to smoke despite, or in the absence of, medical advice may face serious, even fatal, health consequences. Alcoholism causes liver damage, and sometimes failure, resulting in death; injecting drugs increases the risk of fatal overdose and transmission of serious viral infections such as HIV and hepatitis C. Most addictive behaviours take a heavy toll on the individual's relationships and employment prospects.

Why do people become addicts?

Some people try smoking, drinking and recreational drugs as part of an adolescent rebellious phase, only to abandon them when they get older. Others will develop an occasional or regular habit, and a few of these will become addicted. The same is true of addictive behaviours. While one person may enjoy an occasional flutter on the horses, another takes their gambling to extremes and finds themselves in serious financial problems. Is there something intrinsically different about the addict, or is it just a matter of circumstance – they happened to be in the wrong place at the wrong time? Are there differences between those who become addicted to, say nicotine, and those who become addicted to other drugs, such as heroin?

These are fascinating, and important, questions to which, so far, we have only glimpses of an answer. One theory is that there is a strong element of self-medication in taking drugs – that is, addicts have some deficiency within their natural reward circuits that makes them seek out ways of boosting their levels of dopamine or endorphins. Psychiatrist and researcher Dr Avram Goldstein of Stanford University describes how heroin addicts often say that taking the drug made them feel "right" for the first time in their lives.[1] At the biochemical level, this means there may be deficiencies in the neurotransmitters or their receptors that are involved in the reward circuits of the brain, particularly within the mesolimbic dopamine system (see page 35). These deficiencies may be a result of inherited gene mutations. However, no genes that could account for a weak link in the brain's reward circuits have yet been identified.

Is addiction inherited?

The best evidence on the role of genes in addiction comes from the study of alcohol abuse in families.[2] For instance, twin studies can be very revealing about the relative contribution of genes and environment to a condition. Identical twins share the same genetic make-up, while fraternal twins share only half their genes. If genes are entirely responsible for a predisposition to addiction, and environment plays no role, identical twins would be 100 per cent concordant – either predisposed, or not – with respect to alcohol abuse. If environment played a role too, however, the concordance rate would be less than 100 per cent but greater than the concordance in fraternal twins. Data from several countries has shown that for alcoholism, concordance rates between identical twins are less than 100 per cent but still more than those between fraternal twins.

However, there's a flaw in these studies because identical twins brought up together share not only their genes, but also many environmental factors.

Study of dependence among substance users in the US 1990–92[3]

Drug	Adults who have ever used (%)	Adults who are addicted (%)	At risk of addiction (to drug indicated) (%)*
Tobacco	75.6	24.1	31.9
Alcohol	91.5	14.1	15.4
Illicit drugs	51.0	7.5	14.7
Cannabis	46.3	4.2	9.1
Cocaine	16.2	2.7	16.7
Stimulants	15.3	1.7	11.2
Anxiolytics	12.7	1.2	9.2
Analgesics	9.7	0.7	7.5
Psychedelics	10.6	0.5	4.9
Heroin	1.5	0.4	23.1
Inhalants	6.8	0.3	3.7

*% in all three groups refers to percentage of the general population of the USA.

Opiate addiction

 The drug habit becomes an inner need and you have to keep on taking it every day, I don't think I would ever go back to opiates; it takes over your life. No-one gives the drug to you – you have to go and get it, which is hard work. I used to go up West as soon as I finished work and rake around to get what I needed. It took over my life. You lose a lot of weight just worrying whether you will be able to get more drugs. It gets on your nerves.

"Russell", from *Streetwise, Drugwise*, Eva Roman, Richard James, Management Books 2000, 1998

How can we separate the influence of genes and environment?

Robert Cloninger carried out cross-adoption studies that were able to highlight the impact of genes on alcohol addiction. Sons of alcoholics adopted at birth and raised in a non-alcoholic family had a four times higher probability of becoming alcoholic than their stepbrothers. And the sons of non-alcoholic parents, raised in an alcoholic family tended not to become alcoholic, even though their stepbrothers did.

Research on the sons of alcoholics – carried out when they were young enough not to have developed a dependence on drink – shows their brains may already differ from those of sons from non-alcoholic families. They were given low and high doses of alcohol and their mental ability was evaluated with tests. Those from the alcoholic families showed less disruption of performance by the alcohol.[4] This suggests that their brains may have some inbuilt insensitivity to alcohol.

Half of all Japanese and Chinese people carry a gene mutation which makes them intolerant of alcohol; if they drink they develop a facial flush, a severe headache and sometimes more serious reactions.[5] The rate of alcoholism in Japan and China is low. Although there is controversy over the role played by the mutation, its rate among Japanese alcoholics is much lower than among the population as a whole.

In a recent report, researchers at the University of Illinois at Chicago have suggested that a deficiency in the CREB gene might be linked to alcohol abuse.[6] They were studying mice that had only one copy of CREB, rather than the usual two. The genetically deficient mice chose alcohol over water in experiments and were highly anxious during a maze-learning task. (Many people who drink to excess do so because of anxiety or depression.) When CREB is activated, it regulates production of a brain protein called neuropeptide Y. Low levels of both CREB and neuropeptide Y are linked with anxiety and excessive alcohol consumption. In this investigation, the anxiety of the animals was relieved by taking alcohol. This seems to suggest that one explanation for alcohol abuse is a genetic deficiency in CREB.

What's the current thinking on addiction?

Increasingly, addiction is being regarded as a physical disease of the brain. It has long been known that addictive substances are powerful stimulants to the brain's reward systems. More recently, brain imaging and other advanced scientific techniques have shown that chronic exposure to addictive substances can cause short- and long-term changes to the genes, proteins, cells and circuits of the brain. These changes produce tolerance and intensify the substance-seeking behaviour. Advances in understanding the biology of addiction have opened the door to effective ways of dealing with addiction, such as new drug treatments, including vaccines.

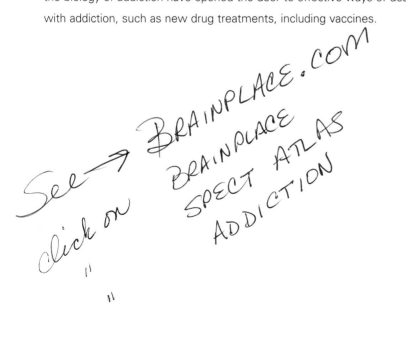

What is a psychoactive substance?

Much of what we understand about addiction comes from research on how psychoactive substances act on the brain. A psychoactive drug is a substance that can alter your state of consciousness, mood or thought processes through the way it acts upon the brain. Caffeine is a psychoactive substance, aspirin is not. All addictive drugs are psycho-active substances but not all psychoactive drugs are addictive.

The main groups are:

- alcohol and other hypnotics or sedatives, nicotine, opiates (like morphine and heroin)
- stimulants (caffeine, cocaine, amphetamine)
- hallucinogens, (such as LSD).

Antidepressants are psychoactive drugs but are not thought to lead to dependence or addiction (although there is some debate). A further complication is that not everyone will become dependent on drugs with the potential for addiction. Many people can happily limit their intake of alcohol, and even powerfully addictive substances do not create dependence in everyone who tries them. LSD and cannabis, for example, are not especially addictive on their own. It is the combination of the substance, circumstances and the individual's predisposition that leads to addiction.

Brain research has shown that most psychoactive drugs act on the brain in the same way as neurotransmitters – the brain's own messengers – activating pathways that lead to a pleasurable experience, such as relaxation, stimulation or enhanced awareness.

The main classes of psychoactive drugs and their effects on the brain

Class of drug	Effect on the brain	Examples
Depressants	Depress the physical functions of the brain and other parts of the central nervous system	Alcohol Barbiturates Benzodiazepines Solvents and gases (e.g. butane lighter fuel)
Stimulants	Excite the brain and central nervous system	Cocaine, Ecstasy, Amphetamines Nicotine Caffeine Alkyl nitrites
Painkillers	Reduce pain, increase pleasure through release of body's own natural painkillers	Opiates (natural derivatives of the opium poppy – morphine, heroin, codeine) Opioids (synthetic drugs with effects similar to opiates)*
Hallucinogens	Act on the brain to alter the perception of reality	LSD Magic mushrooms Cannabis Ketamine MDMA PCP

* The terms opioid and opiate are often used interchangeably; another term often used in this context is narcotic.

N.B. This is a broad and simplified categorization of the most commonly used of the psychoactive drugs.

Getting a bigger buzz

All addictive drugs act – directly or indirectly – in the mesolimbic dopamine system (the dopamine-fuelled neural circuitry that produces a "rush" of pleasure or anticipation when it is stimulated). Much of their effect depends on how the drug is taken. A rapid onset and an intense effect are more likely to lead to addiction.

Science has advanced rapidly and, once chemists isolated the active ingredient of the cocoa plant, cocaine, it became possible to get a more intense effect by oral ingestion or snorting. It was then found that a solution of cocaine hydrochloride could be injected, to give an even more intense "high" . In the 1980s, crack cocaine – a form that can be vaporized by heating – was introduced. Even inhaling the vapours of crack gives blood levels as high as intravenous injection. Smoking nicotine (see page 52) produces a similarly instant effect and the same may also be true of cannabis, although it appears not to be as addictive as cocaine or nicotine.

What's the harm in psychoactive substances if their use is pleasurable?

People generally use psychoactive substances to gain pleasure or avoid pain. There are many ways, however, in which a psychoactive substance can cause physical, mental and social harm. The substance may be harmful in its own right – especially if used to excess. Some substances, such as morphine or alcohol, for example, can be fatal in overdose. Chronic use can also cause health problems . For instance, long-term alcohol use may cause liver damage. A component that is inextricably linked to a psychoactive substance may be damaging, or the substance may be damaging in itself, or both these things may be true. Injecting drugs such as heroin or morphine directly into the bloodstream carries its own risk of infection with viruses such as HIV or hepatitis C, at the same time the purity and content of illicit drugs bought on the street is unknown. If you don't know what you're putting into your body, then how do you know the risks you are running?

Psychoactive substances can also lead to hazardous behaviour. Driving or operating other machinery under the influence of alcohol can lead to serious, even fatal, accidents. Alcohol and other drugs may fuel violent behaviour or suicide. Using psychoactive drugs can also exacerbate existing health problems. Alcohol use may make depression worse or aggravate a stomach ulcer. Smoking – even passive smoking – is dangerous for people who already have asthma and other lung or heart problems. Some psychoactive drugs also interact with prescription medications, either making them ineffective or causing troublesome side-effects. For instance, there is increasing concern about the effect of mixing cocaine and Viagra (a prescription drug, but one that is readily available on the street) as both can cause heart problems.

Addictive behaviour often leads to neglect of everyday activities and responsibilities causing a range of problems at huge cost to society and to the individual. Addiction can lead to financial problems, criminal behaviour and ultimately loss of employment and freedom/independence as well as broken relationships and related social problems.

What are the main theories of addiction?

There is no single integrated theory of addiction. In this book, we look at addiction mainly from a biological point of view, focusing on what happens in the brain during substance-dependent behaviour. But it's important to realize that there are many other ways of interpreting addictive behaviour. When it comes to formal treatment, success is more likely if the client and the therapist or doctor and patient see addiction in roughly the same terms.

There are currently two main theories about how the addictive brain functions. The first looks at how exposure to psychoactive substances alters the biochemistry of the brain both in the short term and the long term. The second is focused more on heredity and genetics and is based on the observation that some forms of substance misuse, such as alcohol addiction, seem to run in families. Both these theories have been supported by recent scientific advances in brain scanning technology and gene technology.

It is also possible to look at addiction in terms of behavioural psychology. In classical conditioning, for example, an individual may learn to associate a stimulus, such as certain places or people, with drug misuse or a type of addictive behaviour, such as gambling. This derives from the theory developed by the famous Russian psychologist Ivan Pavlov.

Social learning theory may also be relevant to understanding drug addiction. Behaviour is shaped by what we expect to happen as a result of a particular activity. The anticipation of short-term pleasure may outweigh the long-term benefit of giving up the behaviour. The addict may also perceive themselves as being incapable of change.

Elements of these psychological theories form the basis of various types of therapy for addiction (see pages 148–161).

What research is being carried out into addiction?

Future understanding of how addiction works is likely to come from high-tech brain imaging. For instance, one study has shown what happens in the brain when a "labelled" version of cocaine was injected.[7] The label gave off radiation that allowed its progress through the brain to be tracked and relayed to a computer monitor. The resulting set of images showed, quite clearly, that the cocaine molecule binds to a dopamine transporter molecule – an action that leaves more dopamine in the brain's reward system. Such information not only adds to our understanding of drug addiction, it also opens the door to potential treatments for addiction that would work on a molecular level. In the above case, for example, researchers might look for a drug that could stop cocaine from binding to the dopamine transporter.

Imaging can also be used to work out the volume of the brain tissue. In another recent study, imaging was used to show that although alcohol shrinks the brain's volume, this change is reversed during abstinence – a finding which demonstrates the extraordinary plasticity of the brain – that is, its ability to respond to changes in behaviour.[8]

Does personality play a role in addiction?

The role of personality in addiction is already well known. Individuals with personality disorders, for instance, are more likely to have problems with addiction, and certain personality types seem to be pre-disposed towards addictive behaviour. Personality itself is, at least partly, influenced by biological factors such as genetics and brain chemistry, although the relationship is complex. It is not yet clear how brain dysregulation and personality factors might be related to cravings.

People often talk of the "addictive personality" , yet there is little evidence of the existence of such a type.[9] You could speculate that those who experiment with illicit drugs are probably risk takers, non-conformists and, perhaps, too readily influenced by their peers (people almost never take heroin for the first time on their own). Analysis of the psychology and personality of people *after* they have become treated, muddies the interpretation of these studies' findings. Little is known of the psychology of the *potential* addict although one study by Robert Cloninger, who evaluated personality traits among several hundred Swedish 11 year-olds over a subsequent period of 16 years, found that those who displayed impulsivity, novelty-seeking and risk-taking traits were far more likely to have drug problems as young adults.[10]

If personality is involved it is never the only factor. Addiction can affect anyone, but personality, co-existing problems, social status and the availability of drugs clearly play a role. A study of heroin addicts in London showed four distinct "types" .[11] "Stables" were those who worked and had regular income. They took their heroin at home, rarely mixed with other addicts and had few physical or social problems. At the other extreme were the "junkies" – who did not work but supported themselves through crime. This group closely resembled the common stereotype of the addict.

They were highly involved with other addicts and, if they had a partner, he or she was also likely to be a drug user. Junkies generally ate poorly and had other health and social problems. A third group – "loners" – was not involved in criminal activity but neither did this type work, being mainly supported by benefits. They tended to use drugs alone. A fourth category – the "two worlder" – exhibited both "stable" and "junkie" characteristics. These individuals worked, but were also sometimes involved in crime although they were less likely than junkies to be imprisoned.

There are also differences between men and women in drug use – women have, in general, lower levels of usage, are less likely to inject, are more likely to have a drug abusing partner and often have co-existing problems. They are less likely to indulge in multiple drug use. Addictions to alcohol and smoking have no typical personality type, though. Both are relatively cheap and attract people from all socio-economic classes. It is important to remember addicts are individuals and should be treated as such.

What about genes that influence addiction?

Many studies have been carried out on genes that influence dopamine, serotonin and other brain circuits to try to uncover a link with substance and behavioural addiction. For instance, certain variants in the dopamine receptor gene have been linked to alcohol and tobacco dependence, dependence on other psychoactive susbtances, novelty-seeking, obesity and compulsive gambling.[12] However, the genetic and personality factors involved in drug taking will only ever be part of the answer as to why someone takes drugs. Environmental, social and cultural factors play an equally important role. Biology need not be destiny. Someone who thinks they have an addictive personality need not be a victim of this label – they could learn to pursue pleasure in a harmless, creative and productive, way.

Genes can come in slightly different forms or variants (known technically as alleles). It has been found that specific variants of a given gene are sometimes linked to physiological or biochemical differences in the individual.

2 Addiction: effects on the brain

"New research indicates that chronic drug use induces changes in the structure and function of the brain's reward system that last for weeks, months or years after the last fix."

Professor Eric Nestler (Southwestern University) and Professor Robert Malanka (Stanford University), *Scientific American*, March 2004

How does the brain respond to addictive substances?

The brain responds to an addictive substance in different ways. In the short term, the substance powerfully stimulates the brain's natural reward system, creating a pleasurable experience. Over time and with chronic use, changes occur in the brain's circuitry and architecture to keep the addict "hooked" . Put simply, this means drug exposure re-models the brain, so that the relationship between the individual and the drug becomes one of dependence.

Animal experiments going back over 40 years have mimicked the dependent behaviour of human addicts. Rats, mice and non-human primates have been connected to an intravenous line containing drugs, such as cocaine, heroin and amphetamine. The animals can press a lever that will deliver either the drug, an innocuous saline solution or a food pellet. Within days, the animals become addicted, preferring the drug to more normal activities like eating or sleeping. Many will spend all their waking hours pressing the drug lever, even if it means dying of malnutrition or exhaustion. Similar experiments also simulate the human craving for drugs. When placed in a cage where pressing a lever leads to drug delivery, the animal will stop pressing the lever if the drug is removed, but the behaviour is immediately resumed if the animals are given just a taste of the drug, or exposed to a cue that implies the drug will be made available. A cue might be a place or object associated with the drug – such as the cage where the drug is administered.

The electrochemical brain

The best way to understand how the brain works and how it is affected by drugs, is to start with the brain cell, or neuron. The brain has up to 100 billion neurons, supported by glial cells, which are even more numerous.

Each neuron has three parts: the cell body, a long fibre called an axon and numerous small projections called dendrites. Information passes from one neuron to another down the axon of one to the dendrites of another. Given that each axon may divide into many thousands of branches at its terminal and that each neuron has, typically, around 10,000 dendrites, each of which could receive input from many different neurons, the patterns of information flowing through the brain are extremely complex. There are trillions of possible connections. This sounds like a recipe for chaos. How can we possibly make sense of anything?

In fact, each individual neuron makes connections with relatively few others. However, the other neurons it "talks" to are not necessarily close by, in fact they could be in some other region of the brain entirely. Neurons seem to work in circuits that connect different brain regions to form systems, each contributing to various sensations and mental functions. Thus, the mesolimbic dopamine system, which is so important in drug taking and addiction, is made up of neurons from many other brain areas.

The flow of information through the nervous system is electrochemical in nature. Tiny electrical impulses travel down axons, but most of them cannot leap from one neuron to another because there is a gap between them, known as a synapse. Communication across a synapse – and between two neurons – occurs through a flow of chemicals manufactured by the neurons themselves, known as neurotransmitters.

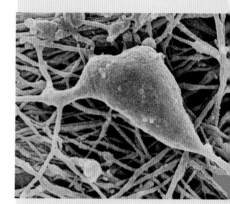

A coloured SEM scan shows a human nerve cell, or neuron. Its dendrites and the cell body are clearly visible.

Neurotransmitters – the brain's messengers

There may be as many as 200 different neurotransmitters in the brain, but only about 50 have been identified (the most important ones, in terms of drug use, are given in the table on page 34). Each one is confined to certain brain circuits that can home in on a range of different receptors – so we talk about "dopamine circuits" or "serotonin circuits" and various types of opioid receptors.

Communication across a synapse is a one-way process. The neurotransmitter flow starts from the pre-synaptic neuron and ends in the post-synaptic neuron. The pre-synaptic neuron releases neurotransmitter molecules into the gap from a small storage compartment called a vesicle. Neurotransmitter molecules travel across a synapse and some of the molecules bind tightly onto receptor molecules on the surface of the post-synaptic neuron, like a key fitting a lock. This binding is like a switch that turns the post-synaptic neuron on or off. There are two types of neurotransmitter – excitatory, which turns a neuron on, and inhibitory, which turns a neuron off. Binding to the receptor is temporary – the neurotransmitter is subsequently cleared away by various mechanisms. Some are broken down by enzymes, while others are recycled by being transported back to the pre-synaptic neuron.*

Levels of neurotransmitter molecules in brain circuits fluctuate, as do the number of receptor molecules available to interact with them. Generally, the brain tries to maintain an equilibrium where excessive stimulation of receptors by neurotransmitters leads to a decrease in the number of receptors, while insufficient stimulation leads to an increase in the number.[13]

Many drugs exert their actions by altering neurotransmitter levels – causing their release from neurons, or preventing their re-uptake.

*Receptor molecules can also be found on the pre-synaptic neurons. Binding to these receptors controls the release of neurotransmitters into the synapse.

As a result, chronic drug exposure may lead to long-term alteration in receptor numbers. Drugs that can activate a neuron through excitation or inhibition when they bind to a receptor are known as agonists; those that merely bind, but do not activate, are called antagonists. Both agonists and antagonists will compete with neurotransmitters and other brain molecules for receptor sites – sometimes with interesting consequences. For instance, if someone takes an overdose of heroin, their life will be endangered if the heroin molecules swamp the opioid receptors in the brain area that controls respiration. However, if the victim is injected with the drug naloxone quickly enough, they may survive; naloxone is an opioid antagonist and will block the opioid receptors so that heroin cannot bind and the receptors cannot activate the neurons involved in respiratory depression.

Neurotransmitters help bridge the gap between neurons, resulting in a chain reaction which enables the nervous system to transmit messages to different parts of the body.

Scanning the brain

Neurotransmitter/ receptor	Normal function	Drugs affecting neurotransmitter
Acetylcholine/ nicotinic and muscarinic	Circuits involved in memory and learning	Nicotine
Gamma- aminobutyric acid (GABA)/GABA-A, GABA-B	Inhibitory neurotransmitter widely distributed throughout the brain	Benzodiazepines, barbiturates and alcohol producing sedation.
Glutamate/NMDA (and other subtypes)	Excitatory neurotransmitter involved in memory and learning	PCP and other hallucinogens
Noradrenaline/ noradrenergic	Circuits involved in stress responses and anxiety	Cocaine and amphetamine increase concentration of noradrenaline. Many antidepressants block re-uptake of noradrenaline
Dopamine/ dopamine	Circuits involved in reward, pleasure, motivation and movement	Most psychoactive drugs
Serotonin/ serotonin	Circuits involved in mood, arousal, impulsiveness, aggression, appetite and anxiety	LSD, MDMA, cocaine, amphetamine, alcohol and nicotine. Many antidepressants block reuptake of serotonin
Endogenous opiates (end- orphins, enkeph- alins)/ opiate	Pain relief, pleasure of food and drugs, relief and anxiety	Opiates e.g. heroin, morphine

What parts of the brain are involved in addiction?

Drugs are powerful stimuli to the brain's reward system – possibly even more powerful than natural stimuli such as food or sex.[14] An essential component of this system is the mesolimbic dopamine system. This involves a group of neurons in the ventral tegmental area (VTA) at the base of the brain, which produce the neurotransmitter dopamine.[15] When dopamine is released from the VTA while a drug is being taken, it makes a connection to another important area in the brain called the nucleus accumbens, just beneath the frontal cortex where planning, reflection and decision making take place. Dopamine molecules bind to receptor molecules on neurons within the NA, and the addict experiences a "high", sometimes known as the dopamine rush. If the mesolimbic dopamine system is removed from experimental animals, they immediately cease their addictive behaviour.[16, 17]

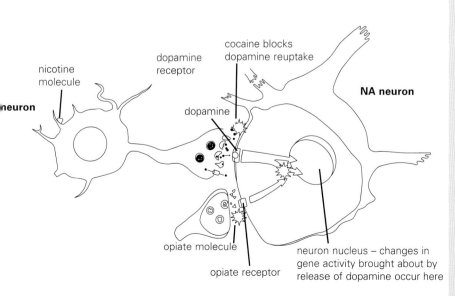

nicotine molecule

neuron

dopamine receptor

cocaine blocks dopamine reuptake

dopamine

NA neuron

opiate molecule

opiate receptor

neuron nucleus – changes in gene activity brought about by release of dopamine occur here

This diagram shows a neuron in the nucleus accumbens (right), and a neuron in the ventral tegmental area. The effect of dopamine release is triggered by many drugs.

The mesolimbic dopamine system is also closely linked with other brain areas. These secondary connections shape our response to drugs and drive ensuing behaviour. The amygdala, for instance, is an important emotional centre, that tells us whether we like or dislike a stimulus, such as drinking alcohol. The hippocampus is involved in memory and learning and stores the memory of where we were and who we were with when we had the experience, playing a role in the creation of cues that might trigger a craving. Contacts with the frontal cortex, a part of the brain concerned with personality, planning, and past experience, add a personal dimension to the event, helping to co-ordinate the whole experience. We can weigh up the pros and cons, take on board advice and information, experience positive and negative emotions, all of which colour the reward we get from a drug or addictive behaviour pattern.

The biology of craving

Craving is perhaps one of the least understood features of addiction. It's best described as a strong (even irrational or uncontrollable) desire or urge for either a substance or a behaviour. Craving is thought to play an important role in the transition to addiction, for example from social drinking to alcoholism. It is clearly important in relapse but the relationship is not simple. Craving doesn't always lead to relapse, and relapse may happen without any preceding craving. Better insight into the biology of craving is important – for both diagnosis and therapy.

Roel Verheul and his team at the Amsterdam Institute for Addiction Research have put forward an interesting model of craving that may help to explain its role in alcohol, cocaine, opiate and nicotine addiction.[18] It takes into account both neurochemical and personality factors and suggests three different dimensions to the craving phenomenon.

Types of cravings

Reward **craving** may involve dysregulation of the dopamine and/or opioid circuits in the brain. Individuals craving alcohol, for example, do so because they anticipate pleasure and reward from achieving their goal. Social drinking may escalate to binge drinking and then to alcohol addiction.

Relief **craving** may be related to the dysregulation of GABA/ glutaminergic brain circuits, which control levels of arousal. Affected individuals may be sensitive to stress and look to the anxiolytic effects of alcohol and other drugs for relaxation, escape and relief. They tend to resort to alcohol as a reaction to adverse events and will drink, possibly alone, to "drown their sorrows".

Obsessive **craving** may involve a deficiency in serotonin levels. Those affected will be prone to obsessive behaviour and find it hard to control their emotions. In the case of alcohol, their drinking will be marked by a compulsiveness and will not be linked to any specific triggers.

Analysing the type of craving experienced by an individual can be an important step in deciding the most appropriate therapy. For instance, someone whose alcohol craving has an obsessive character is more likely to be helped by an SSRI, which will raise their serotonin levels, than by naltrexone, an opioid antagonist used to treat alcohol dependence. Yet so far, these ideas haven't been proven in clinical practice.

Does addiction have a long-term effect on the brain?

Chronic drug and alcohol users develop tolerance, dependence and withdrawal symptoms – three closely related biological phenomena – if their drug of choice is removed. Research suggests that chronic exposure to drugs actually leads to suppression of the brain's reward circuitry – so more drugs are needed to get the same effect, leading to dependence, drug-seeking activities, and mental and physical discomfort during withdrawal.

Put simply, when dopamine levels rise in the nucleus accumbens,(NA) levels of a small – but very important – "signalling" molecule called cyclic AMP go up too. This makes another molecule, spring into action – switching on specific genes that have the overall effect of "damping down" the reward circuit. Next time you take the drug, you'll need more to achieve the same plesurable intensity – it's as if the reward circuit needs more of a kick-start to get it going.

A second kind of molecular gene switch plays a role in longer term drug use and in relapse. This molecular switch stays active for weeks or even months after drug taking, causing long-term alterations in the brain's circuits. Mice with high levels of this substance in their brain are prone to relapsing into drug taking – so we know this must be an important molecule in understanding how addiction acts in the brain. It even looks as if this molecule may alter the actual architecture of cells in the nucleus accumbens, causing them to grow new branch-like structures called "dendritic spines" that contain receptors (docking points) for dopamine. This has the effect of making the whole reward system hypersensitive to drugs. For the alcohol abuser, just one drink is enough to trigger this hypersensitivity and lead to a relapse. Cocaine and amphetamines can also produce sensitization.

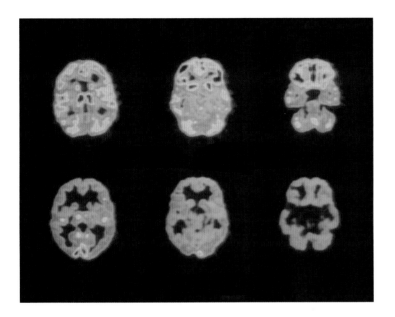

Horizontal sections of a normal brain (top) and a brain four months after heavy cocaine use (bottom) are shown. The front of the brains are at the top of the image, and the slices of the brain get deeper from left to right. The brighter (yellow) areas of the brain show those areas of high activity. The brain of the cocaine user is seen to be less active than the healthy brain, even after four months of abstinence.

In coloured positron emission tomography (PET) scans, radioactively-tagged molecules are injected into the bloodstream and their emissions monitored. Glucose is used here, as it is taken up by active brain cells. The scans show the brain metabolism of a healthy subject (top row) and a cocaine abuser four months coming off the drug. The images above show that in the case of cocaine, long-term changes in the way the brain behaves are clearly visible.

3 Alcohol and addiction

"By winter 1993, I no longer drank to get drunk nor did I drink to medicate my problems. I only drank for one reason: to feel normal. I didn't enjoy drinking anymore. It wasn;t even fun."

Nick Johnstone, *A Head Full of Blue,* **Bloomsbury, 2002**

Why is alcohol so popular?

Alcohol is one of the most readily available and widely consumed drugs in the world. Ninety per cent of the British population, for example, drinks to some degree, even if only occasionally. Alcohol plays a central role in social and ceremonial occasions. Wines, beers and spirits are also valued for their taste unlike any other psychoactive beverage, except perhaps caffeine-containing tea and coffee. More people are addicted to alcohol than any other drug except nicotine. This doesn't necessarily mean it is more addictive *per se*, merely that its widespread availability creates more opportunities for addiction.

Alcohol is a psychoactive drug, but its effects on an individual's behaviour depend on many factors, including the following:

- alcohol content of the drink
- rate of drinking
- social context
- gender
- body weight
- time elapsed since the last drink.

This explains why the behaviour and experience of a group of family and friends enjoying a bottle of wine or two with a relaxed lunch might be very different to that of a crowd of football fans in a pub caught up in the emotion of the big game. The impact of alcohol will vary not only between these groups but also among the individuals within the group.

Alcohol is almost always taken by mouth, which means there's a delay of at least a few minutes before its effects are felt. It is absorbed into the bloodstream from the small intestine and drinking with or after food will slow the absorption of alcohol.

What are the physical effects of alcohol?

The effects of alcohol depend on the level present in the bloodstream. With low levels – for example 50 mg per centilitre, from just one or two drinks – you experience pleasant effects such as relaxation and loosening of inhibitions. If you continue drinking, less pleasant effects may become apparent, such as lack of co-ordination, slurring of speech and emotional instability. Very heavy consumption, resulting in blood levels of 500–800 mg per centilitre can be fatal, although most people would probably pass out before reaching this level.

As alcohol passes through the stomach and liver, it is broken down into acetaldehyde by an enzyme (biological catalyst) called alcohol dehydrogenase (ADH). Acetaldehyde is the substance responsible for the symptoms of a hangover, especially headache. The liver breaks down acetaldehyde into acetate using a second enzyme called acetaldehyde dehydrogenase. This process actually takes several hours, which is why you don't usually get a hangover until the morning after a night of heavy drinking. Women have lower levels of these alcohol breakdown enzymes than men, which is why they're more vulnerable to the effects of alcohol.

People quickly become tolerant to alcohol – someone who rarely drinks will find that a glass of champagne at a wedding "goes straight to their head" while a more seasoned drinker will need several glasses to experience the same impact. This happens, in part, because levels of the breakdown enzymes increase with frequent consumption, meaning that more is needed to get the same effect. Heavy users of alcohol are also prone to withdrawal symptoms – shaking, sweating, headache and even seizures. Withdrawal may be complicated by a neurological condition called delirium tremens (DTs) with hallucinations, delusions and severe agitation.

What does alcohol do to the brain?

All the aspects of withdrawal are related to how alcohol acts on the brain.

Alcohol acts as a depressant. This doesn't (necessarily) mean that it makes you feel sad. In terms of how the brain works, it dampens down the activity of neurons. Alcohol depresses brain activity by acting on inhibitory circuits powered by a neurotransmitter called gamma-amino butyric acid (GABA). It also decreases activity in circuits that are usually excitatory, powered by another group of neurotransmitters called glutamate receptors.

The addictive properties of alcohol, however, are related to its action in the mesolimbic dopamine system where it inhibits neurons in the VTA that would otherwise block the release of dopamine.[19] Like other powerfully addictive drugs, it enhances the action of the mesolimbic dopamine system. Alcohol's effect on mood may also be linked to the changes it causes in noradrenaline and serotonin levels.[20] For someone who is prone to depression, alcohol can provide a quick lift, because it increases serotonin levels (serotonin is often referred to as the "feel good" chemical of the brain). But serotonin levels fall again once the drinking stops and a depressed person may feel even worse. There is a complex relationship between alcohol, depression, suicide and violence and we still don't know whether depression leads to alcohol abuse or vice versa.[21] It seems to be a complex partnership and one that depends on the individual (see page 48).

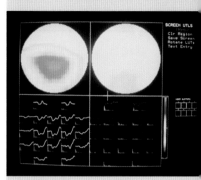

A Coloured Evoked Potential brain scan shows areas of electrical activity in a normal and alcoholic patient. Areas of electrical activity in the brain are colour-coded: low activity (blue), high activity (yellow, red). The front of the brain is at top. At left is the brain of a normal patient with high activity in the posterior region. At right, the alcoholic patient shows depressed brain activity. The coloured graph shows EEG (electro-encephalogram) readings made using electrodes on the scalp, and then used to construct these brain scans.

Brain wave patterns in alcoholics

Most diagnoses of alcohol – and other addiction – problems still centre
on giving the individual a questionnaire about their intake and habits. There
are few tests of brain function that can reveal an addiction – although this
is likely to change with advances in imaging research. However, there is
evidence that alcoholics have a subtle abnormality of information
processing that is revealed by their brain wave patterns.[22]

The neuropsychological test used depends on measuring a peak of
electrical activity called P300. In this test, the subject sits quietly listening
to a regular series of sounds while their brain waves are recorded by an
electroencephalography (EEG). The sounds are presented randomly, with a
"target" higher-pitched tone and the subject is told to raise their finger
when they hear it. Analysis of the EEG trace shows a peak appearing 300
milliseconds after the target tone is sounded – this is the P300 peak.
Psychologists believe that this peak is a indicator of the information
processing that goes on in the brain between hearing the order to raise the
finger and actually carrying out the action.

Alcohol has been shown to reduce the size of the P300 peaks – but to a
lesser extent in alcoholics, which suggests they are less sensitive to
alcohol (a finding that's been borne out in other research). Moreover,
abstinent alcoholics and the sons (and other relatives) of alcoholics show
reduced P300 which suggests that there is some innate abnormality of
brain function that predisposes someone towards alcohol abuse. This is
probably related to a genetic factor, although the specific genes – possibly
involving dopamine or serotonin metabolism – are proving hard to identify.

What is sensible drinking?

Until 1995, the so-called "sensible limits" on weekly alcohol consumption given by the UK government were the following (where a unit is a standard drink containing about eight grams of alcohol – a half pint of ordinary strength beer, a single measure of spirits (25ml) or a small (125ml) glass of wine).

not more than 21 units for men
14 units for women

Of course, beer and wine vary greatly in their alcoholic strength, so these measures were only guidelines. Some wine labels now contain information on how many units you get in a 125 ml glass. In 1995, the government revised the sensible limits to 3–4 units a day for men and 2–3 units a day for women (with the caution that regular consumption of 4 units a day for men and 3 for women is not recommended on health grounds). There is an upper limit of weekly alcohol consumption – of 50 units for men and 35 for women where health is very likely to be impaired. Levels between the upper and lower limit are linked to increasing hazard.

Where do the alcohol guidelines come from? Much research has been conducted on the effect of alcohol on health and, overall, it shows that light drinking does not pose much harm and may even do good in relieving stress and protecting from heart disease, although these benefits may be more relevant to older people. Strictly speaking, the limits are not really "safe drinking" limits. They are the levels of regular consumption below which adults are *relatively* unlikely to be at risk of illness or premature death. Doctors are, understandably, reluctant to be seen to be encouraging drinking so, officially, there is no "safe" limit of alcohol consumption.

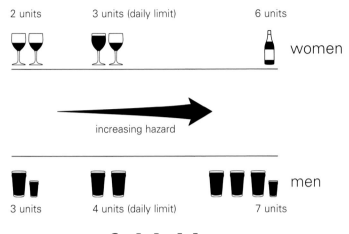

2 units   3 units (daily limit)   6 units   women

increasing hazard

men

3 units   4 units (daily limit)   7 units

The current recommended sensible limit for daily drinking is three units a day for women (three small glasses of wine or one and a half pints of beer) and four units for men (four small glasses of wine or two pints of beer). Previously, these limits were two and three units respectively. Increasing intake beyond sensible limits is linked to increasing health risk.

Patterns of drinking

Ongoing research from the World Health Organization (WHO) reveals that there are wide variations between countries in both the amount of alcohol consumed and the context in which it is drunk. These drinking patterns are relevant to the incidence of alcohol abuse.

In the Eastern Mediterranean, which includes Afghanistan and Pakistan, 83 per cent of men and 99 per cent of women abstain from alcohol. Here, the average per capita consumption of alcohol per annum is only 0.8 litres. The few who drink, consume an average of 8.9 litres per person per year. In France, Germany and the UK, abstention is far less common – only ten per cent of men and 19 per cent of women don't drink.[23] Average consumption is 13.0 litres per person per year, for the population as a whole. Among those who do drink, average consumption is 15.2 litres per person per year. The WHO also distinguishes four drinking patterns – with 1, where drinking is done socially with meals, seen as the least detrimental, and 4, where heavy drinking outside meal times is the norm, being most hazardous. In Africa, Latin America and the Western Pacific, binge drinking, especially in men, is not uncommon. Similarly, in Eastern Europe, there is more heavy binge drinking. But in Western Europe, with the possible exception of the UK, Type 1 drinking is more likely.

When drinking becomes a problem

Type of consumption	Medical problems	Psychological/ social problems
Intoxication (being under the influence of alcohol)	Alcohol poisoning (occasionally fatal), gastritis, disturbed sleep	Unsafe sex, drunken driving, accidents, homicide
Alcohol abuse (a pattern of drinking which, while harmful, falls short of dependence)	Liver damage, brain damage, high blood pressure, heart disease, cancer	Absence from work, marital problems, criminal behaviour, sexual dysfunction, depression
Alcohol dependence (equivalent to alcohol addiction)	Dementia, hallucinations, withdrawal, including delerium tremens	Social disintegration, paranoia, relationship problems, financial problems, unemployment, homelessness

Too much alcohol on one occasion or over a period of time can lead to various physical and psychological/social problems that are summed up in the table to the left.

Are you an alcoholic?

Do you drink too much?

Doctors and nurses sometimes use the CAGE questionnaire to detect drinking problems in adults and adolescents over 16. It is accurate, brief and non-confrontational.[24] These are the four questions:

- Have you ever felt you should CUT DOWN your drinking?

- Have people ANNOYED you by criticizing your drinking?

- Have you ever felt bad or GUILTY about your drinking?

- Have you ever had a drink first thing in the morning to steady your nerves or get rid of a hangover (EYE-OPENER).

Alcohol dependence is thought likely if the patient gives two or more positive answers.

4 Smoking

"Nobody has yet been able to demonstrate to me how I can join words into whole sentences on a blank page without a cigarette burning away between my lips."

Dennis Potter, playwright, *The Sunday Times*, 30th October 1977

Are you hooked on smoking?

One smoker in three becomes addicted to nicotine according to a large survey of drug use carried out in the USA.[25] This makes it more addictive than any other known drug, including alcohol and heroin.

Deep inhalation and frequency of smoking are the key to nicotine dependence. Smoke from a cigarette enters the tiny air sacs in the lungs where it rapidly passes into the network of fine capillaries surrounding them and into the blood supply feeding the brain. At each puff, the brain receives a powerful "spike" of nicotine. What is more, the smoker has control over administration of the nicotine, though it's notable that people smoking cigarettes that are lower in nicotine and tar tend to inhale more deeply to get the same hit.

Nicotine gives a gentle "high" compared to other drugs. It relieves stress and increases attention and concentration. It also suppresses appetite in the short-term. Nicotine stays in the body for about two hours – after which time it is broken down and excreted in the urine. In some people, this process takes a bit longer than usual and it's been found that tobacco addiction is less likely in this group (probably because the effect of a cigarette is longer-lasting so they don't feel the need to light up so often).[26]

Tolerance to nicotine develops rapidly, which may be why most smokers say the first cigarette of the day is the most pleasurable (there is more impact per puff compared to the effect of cigarettes smoked later). The appeal of the first cigarette may also be because it relieves the withdrawal symptoms caused by nicotine levels in the blood falling overnight. The urge to smoke certainly correlates with low blood nicotine levels. Withdrawal leads to irritability, anxiety, depression and increased appetite.

The quitter's story

I started smoking when I was 15 years old. I had a boyfriend who smoked and he used to laugh at me, saying that I didn't smoke properly because I didn't inhale! A lot of my friends smoked too and at college one or two of them tried to stop. I remember that they were absolutely astounded at how difficult it was. I remained a heavy smoker throughout my 20s, sometimes smoking as many as 60 cigarettes a day.

I tried loads of quit techniques over the years. I used those filters that are supposed to reduce the amount you take in from your cigarettes, but they didn't help much and I soon went back to my normal smoking pattern. I tried those ghastly herbal cigarettes that contain no nicotine. They were awful! There was no nicotine, so no satisfaction or craving relief, plus they smelled like a bonfire in June.

When I was 30, the relationship I was in broke up. I'd managed to stop smoking a short while before but then, when things seemed to be falling apart, I thought, "I'll just buy one packet to get me through this week." I was soon smoking heavily again and went on to suffer a nervous breakdown. I was very unwell and it seemed as though my life was disintegrating, so I clung to my cigarettes during those difficult times.

The more times I tried to quit, the more I learned about tobacco addiction. I started to collect snippets of information about smoking from magazines, newspapers and books and as time went by it turned into a sort of bizarre hobby! Smoking affects so many different parts of the body and the more I found out, the more I wanted to know. I think I was subconsciously trying to put myself off tobacco by learning all about its effects. Then I had the idea of putting all the information I'd collected into a book that someone could carry about with them – a kind of "book of willpower" they could look at when they needed to feel positive about quitting.

I put out my last cigarette whilst in the course of writing the book, and although I hadn't told myself that I was going to quit, something clicked. I just didn't go and buy any more when I ran out. The first week was pretty awful because I was violently irritable, but after about four or five days I calmed down and began to believe that I really could do it. I think a lot of people who suffer from depression tend to self-medicate with cigarettes, so it was vital to break the link between feeling bad and smoking.

From ASH website, formerly in *STOP* magazine

Smokers lose a decade of life

It is 50 years since Richard Doll and his team at the University of Oxford first warned of the health risks of smoking. Now, we have a full picture of what has happened to those who took up smoking during the 20th century, and the impact of giving up.

Doll's updated report is a 50-year follow-up of a group of 34,439 British male doctors who entered the study in 1951.[27] Doctors are a group particularly easy to track over time and the study has provided much useful data. Those born between 1900 and 1930 who continued to smoke, lost, on average, ten years of life to smoking-related disease (mainly heart disease, lung disease or cancer). In effect, this means that smoking kills around half of those who continue, mainly in middle age. For doctors born around 1920, the toll exerted by smoking was greater still – they were three times more likely to die than non-smokers between the age of 35 and 69, if they did not give up. This might have been because these men were conscripted into the British army during World War II, and were provided with low cost cigarettes to help them deal with the stress of combat. *The British Medical Journal* itself was even carrying advertisements for cigarettes in 1950, the year before this study began.

What about those doctors who gave up smoking? The study shows that giving up at ages 60, 50, 40 or 30 gains back three, six, nine or the full ten years of that decade lost to those who carry on smoking. Overall, tobacco has caused six million deaths in Britain over the last 50 years, but, as the message of the Doll studies has spread, more and more people have given up and mortality from smoking-related disease has declined significantly in the UK. Worldwide, however, the death toll may soon reach six million *a year*.

How I gave up smoking

 My first ever smoke was when I was at college in India in 1956. I was 18 at the time. My parents would have disapproved, but I didn't smoke in front of them. My wife doesn't drink or smoke but I remember my grandmother had a hubble-bubble pipe. When she was getting old and dying (I was 4 or 5 at the time), my father would say "Look! That's what's killing you". She sometimes used to send me to get her tobacco for her so that he wouldn't know about it.

When I came to Britain in 1961, I bought 200 duty-free cigarettes, which got me into the habit of daily smoking. I came to study mining engineering and went on to work in the mines. The work is very hard, but one good thing about mining is that you're not allowed to take cigarettes down the pit! As soon as we came out, we were always desperate for a smoke.

It was after a hospital visit about two years ago that I finally decided to quit. They had found some liquid in my lungs so they drained it out and did an endoscopy. The consultant said that I had a tumour in one lung, but that he wouldn't operate if I didn't stop smoking. On the way out, one of the nurses gave me some leaflets on giving up smoking, but I was upset and frightened, so the first thing I did was to go out to the car and roll myself a cigarette!

When I'd calmed down, I got in touch with Christine Hewitt at BRASS (Bradford Smoking Cessation Service). Christine advised me on all the different treatment methods available. I used nicotine patches for a while, but then I carried on without them and I managed to resist the desire to smoke. I was a bit irritable at times, but when the cravings were bad I'd eat or chew spicy things like cloves. They have a very bitter taste and for some reason that seemed to help. It took about six to nine weeks for the cravings to go away completely.

When I went back to the hospital, they did a second scan and I waited nervously for the results, but when they came, it turned out that I didn't have a tumour after all! I wasn't angry about the mistake. It had at least made me decide to quit smoking and that may well save me from having problems later on.

My breathing is easier these days and I can taste my food much more. My wife is proud of me for doing so well. It's two years since I quit and I'd like to thank Christine and the staff at BRASS for all their help and encouragement.

From ASH website, formerly in *STOP* magazine

What does nicotine do to the brain?

Nicotine acts as a stimulant and binds to receptors called nicotinic receptors in several parts of the brain.[28] It has also been found to increase dopamine levels in the nucleus accumbens. Studies have shown that blocking dopamine release stops rats from self-administering nicotine – a standard way to investigate whether a drug is addictive.[29] In experiments this is done by giving a rat a drug that acts on the brain so that dopamine isn't released and the reward circuit is effectively "disabled". In such an experiment carried out with cocaine, the drug does not give its usual end result, by acting on this circuit, so the animal loses interest in the drug. Despite this theory, it was believed for a long time that nicotine was not addictive because it wasn't possible to get rats to press a lever for it. This may be because first exposure to nicotine is often unpleasant – many people will recall feeling sick or having a racing heart when they first smoked a cigarette. For some, this deters for life, but many others go on to develop a full-blown addiction by gradually building tolerance. This kind of behaviour has since been found to occur in experimental rats. [30]

In the short term, nicotine itself causes few problems and some even maintain that it sharpens mental faculties.[31] But in the long term, nicotine damages the heart and circulation because it causes the blood vessels to narrow. And other substances in tobacco, like carbon monoxide and a range of carcinogens, increase the risk of heart disease and cancer.

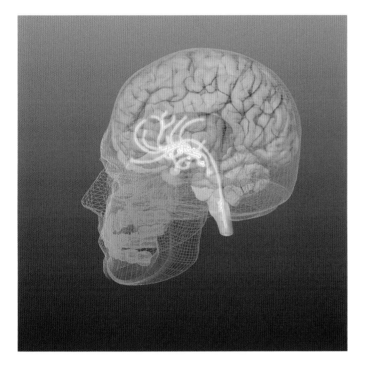

Dopamine pathways in the brain are thought to be affected by nicotine in a similar way to how other drugs act on the brain. This picture shows the dopamine pathways spreading widely through the brain. Dopamine controls arousal levels in many parts of the brain and is vital for giving physical motivation.

5 Hidden addictions and everyday habits

"And...the shops. Shop after shop after shop. Ferragamo. Valentino. Dior. Versace. Prada. As I venture down the street my head swivelling from side to side, I feel giddy."

Sophie Kinsella, *Shopaholic and Sister***, Bantam, 2004**

Can food be addictive?

Food is a natural stimulus for the brain's reward systems. Put very simply, if eating weren't pleasurable, we might not bother and then we wouldn't survive. There are certainly some parallels between eating problems and drug addictions, with compulsion and craving playing an important role in each. This has been shown by at least one study of so-called "chocolate addicts".[32]

A group of self-identified "chocoholics" in the northeast of Scotland was compared to a group that liked chocolate, but did not consider themselves addicted to it. On exposure to chocolate cues – seeing it and smelling it – the chocoholics became more emotionally aroused in terms of feeling excitement, craving, frustration, anxiety and guilt. When both groups were allowed to eat as much chocolate as they wanted – the chocoholics consumed about two and a half times as much as the non-chocoholics (an average of 112 grams compared to 45 grams). The chocoholics were also more likely to be depressed and to have a tendency towards disordered eating patterns. (This raises the interesting question: do people eat chocolate to cheer themselves up when they feel down – what comes first, depression or dependence?) So self-identified chocolate addicts do, indeed, share some of the emotional responses and psychological characteristics of addicts to other substances.

Craving for certain foods, like chocolate, ice-cream, pastry or curry, is common and differs from normal food choices or appetite. Women are more prone than men to report cravings for chocolates and sweets although these sensations decline with age (as do cravings for drugs).[33] Food cravings can lead to disordered eating behaviour – excessive snacking, bingeing and not eating a balanced diet. However, they may also help people to eat a more varied diet, with a better chance of getting all the nutrients they need, because cravings seem to increase among those on a monotonous diet.[34]

There is certainly a link between sweets and drugs. Animals that self-administer drugs are also drawn towards sweet foods, especially if they are under stress.[35] Sweets are said to help with withdrawal from drugs such as heroin, and people abstaining from alcohol often report an increased craving for sweet foods. It's also not uncommon for smokers to put on weight after quitting because they turn to sweets as a substitute. The sensation of sweetness – from whatever source, not just sugar – has been giving pleasure for thousands of years.[36] Therefore sugar-free sweets and sugar substitutes should be able to satisfy cravings as well as sugar itself, for those who want to cut calories.

Can food act like a drug?

It's no surprise to learn from experiments with rats that foods that are craved can act rather like alcohol and heroin in the brain, stimulating the release of the body's natural opioids, the endorphins – a natural phenomenon already known to play an important part in the pleasure of eating.[37] Another study has shown that a high-fat diet alters brain chemistry in a similar way. [38]

Researchers at Princeton University fed rats a diet with increasing amount of sugar and found that the more they were given, the quicker they ate it. If they were treated with naloxone, an opioid antagonist (used in the treatment of heroin addiction), they experienced symptoms such as teeth chattering, anxiety and shaking – all highly suggestive that sugar can induce a state similar to opioid dependence.[39]

Carbohydrate, especially in the absence of protein, may stimulate the release of the neurotransmitter serotonin; this is because carbohydrates are a source of the amino acid tryptophan, which is readily converted into serotonin in the brain. Serotonin levels are often lowered in depression and people who are depressed sometimes report carbohydrate cravings – this may be an attempt to self-medicate this imbalance (as, indeed, may be the case in a great deal of drug misuse).[40]

Eating behaviour (like sexual behaviour) is complex and still not completely understood. Whether food addiction really exists – in the way we understand addiction – is still not clear. Our brains are programmed to find foods high in fat and sugar palatable because they are high in calories. In the days when humans were more physically active this had real survival value, providing the energy to perform everyday activities. In today's more sedentary society a high-calorie diet can lead to obesity and increased risk of premature death from diabetes, heart disease and cancer.

Why does caffeine give you a lift?

Caffeine is a stimulant – it gets you going in the morning and keeps you awake at night. Its half-life in the body is about five to six hours, which is why it's worth cutting out caffeine after around 4pm if you find it hard to sleep. However, the action of caffeine in the brain differs from that of stimulants, such as cocaine and amphetamine. Caffeine doesn't directly stimulate the brain, but it inhibits the dampening of neurons that naturally induce sleep.

All cellular activity is driven by a biochemical fuel called ATP (adenosine triphosphate). There is more ATP around in the brain during waking hours, because there is more neuronal activity. When ATP is used up, it produces adenosine as a waste product. So during the day, when cells are more active, adenosine accumulates. It docks onto adenosine receptors, especially on two small patches of cells in the brain stem, where there are lots of these receptors. These cells are linked to the rest of the brain in such a way that when they become quiet, activity dies down all over, encouraging sleep. During the night, adenosine levels fall, because there is less neuronal activity and therefore less ATP around. The receptors become unoccupied by adenosine molecules and the "brake" lifts, nudging the brain into wakefulness.

The caffeine molecule and adenine (the part of adenosine that locks onto the receptor) belong to the same chemical family – the purines – and are similar in shape and structure. Caffeine can occupy adenosine's space on the adenosine receptor and so block its braking action on the cell. Instead of feeling sleepy, the brain stays alert.

The most popular drug in the world?

Caffeine is one of the most widely-used psychoactive drugs in the world. It is the main active ingredient in tea and coffee and is found in over 100 different plant species. The related stimulants theophylline and theobromine occur in the cocoa plant, from which chocolate is made. Coffee contains about 100 milligrams of caffeine per average cup; tea maybe half as much. And a square of chocolate contains as much stimulant in the form of caffeine, theophylline and theobromine as a cup of tea. Caffeine is added to various soft drinks, as well as being a component of some pain medications. Caffeine pills are also available without prescription.

Is caffeine addictive?

The short answer is, no. Caffeine is not involved in the mesolimbic dopamine pathway so is not a classic drug of addiction, but it shares many of the characteristics of addictive substances (see page 20–21), and many people report reactions to it that are almost identical to a "classic" addiction.

Caffeine is a remarkably safe drug, but it does have a few unwanted side-effects. It increases heart rate and high doses may produce palpitations in certain susceptible people. These symptoms may be alarming but are generally not harmful. Caffeine also leads to increased frequency of urination. You would have to drink over 100 cups of coffee to ingest a possibly lethal dose. There have been occasional reports of people dying by consuming large numbers of caffeine tablets. People talk about trying to "wean themselves off" coffee. When they feel dependent on caffeine and uncomfortable when they withdraw from it, there are some well-known withdrawal symptoms, such as: headaches and feeling less alert. People can also become tolerant and need more caffeine to get the same "buzz" (see page 22).

WHAT ABOUT CHOCOLATE??!

Can behaviours such as gambling, shopping or internet use be addictive?

There is a compulsive aspect to certain behaviours – sex, gambling, work, and surfing the internet, for example – that bears at least a superficial resemblance to drug addiction. Many people, including well-known public figures and celebrities, are more willing to talk about their problems and reveal their own addictions. This has led to a widening – and perhaps trivializing – of the concept of addiction. There are, for example, 26 self-help groups for different addictions in the UK modelled on the concept of Alcoholics Anonymous, including Sex Addicts Anonymous, Workaholics Anonymous and Helpers Anonymous.[41] It is not clear whether these "addictions" can be diagnosed using the same clinical criteria as for heroin or alcohol addiction. However there is some evidence that leads to the suggestion that these behaviours activate the same pathways as a drug addiction. Much of what we understand about substance abuse has come from studies of laboratory animals who can be induced to self-administer a substance. Behavioural addictions are less easy to test for in this manner, nevertheless, it's possible that brain imaging studies carried out on human subjects will shed more light on behavioural addictions. There is little doubt that compulsive behaviour causes much suffering and those involved deserve support and treatment. Whether it is helpful to call such behaviours "addictions" is a relatively unimportant question.

What kinds of behaviours can be addictive?

Some of the behaviours thought to be addictive are listed below:

Sport/exercise

A mild addiction to exercise might be thoroughly beneficial. Intense and sustained physical activity releases natural brain chemicals called endorphins which can lead to the "runner's high" and regular exercise can only benefit your physical and mental health (that's why we're all being urged to take more exercise). Professional athletes may seem to be addicted in a more serious way to their exercise routines but this can be rationalized by their goals – a gold medal, a personal best, winning the race of a lifetime. A few people, however, seem driven to exercise far more than is necessary for their health, without having any particular sporting target in mind other than a compulsion to continue. When exercise takes priority over everything else, the person could have a problem. Although rare, exercise addiction has been linked to eating disorders.[42]

Work

Of all the behavioural addictions, work addiction is perhaps the least likely to be considered a problem by most people. Society respects those who work hard for their money and few people admit to getting pleasure from work. But for some people the stress of juggling several work targets or deadlines creates an adrenaline high than can be addictive in the broadest sense of the word. When people work excessively long hours, when there's no real pressure to do so, and neglect other aspects of their life, there's a danger they may be dependent on their jobs for fulfilment.

Overwork can affect your physical and mental health. It can even kill – in Japan, 10,000 deaths a year are attributed to overwork. There is even a special term for it – karachi.[43]

Sex

Sex is a pleasurable activity so it's not surprising that it has the potential for addiction. It's not known how many people are "sex addicts" but tell-tale signs include: a need to "escape" after sexual activity, having risky or unsafe sex regularly, feeling empty or unsatisfied after sex, getting into trouble because of sexual activity (for example, under-age sex, exhibitionism or voyeurism), having sex in places or with people you wouldn't normally choose.[44]

Internet

The internet is becoming increasingly important in many people's lives and there's concern that certain aspects, such as chat-rooms, may be addictive. One survey showed that six per cent of those questioned felt they were addicted and 30 per cent felt some guilt over their internet use.[45] Withdrawal symptoms from internet use, such as irritability and moodiness when access to the web is denied, have been reported. Many addicts ignore physical symptoms like backache or eye-strain to stay on line. The internet can also be a gateway to other addictions, such as gambling, sex and shopping, because they offer a safe, comfortable and discreet way to indulge.

Shopping

It has never been easier to obtain credit or loans – and having ready access to money can fuel a shopping addiction as easily as cheap cigarettes keep people smoking. One survey suggested that as many as one in four Britons feels they are addicted to shopping.[46] A tell-tale symptom is getting pleasure from the act of shopping itself, rather than the item bought. Often the item will never be used or worn. Another is abnormal feelings of guilt and helplessness mixed with pleasure or euphoria associated with the act of shopping (unusual when you consider that many regard shopping as just an essential everyday chore). And finally, of course, spending beyond one's means nearly always accompanies compulsive shopping.

Gambling

Up to one per cent of the UK population is said to have a problem with gambling – with casinos and sports accounting for most cases and the Lottery the least.[47] Gambling was probably the first behavioural addiction to be taken seriously by health professionals. Like other forms of risk-taking, it involves the prospect of escaping from reality and the ensuing feelings of guilt and helplessness when things don't work out. Compulsive gambling has serious consequences in terms of debt problems.

Text message and mobile phones

Addiction to mobile phones, text messages and the internet are known collectively as "contact addictions" . Recent reports show how some people are now spending up to seven hours a day sending text messages and one had even developed repetitive strain injury.[48] If deprived of their phones, these addicts become moody and irritable.

Risk taking

Most addictive behaviours involve some level of risk taking. But some people seem to get a high – from an adrenaline "rush" – from risk-taking *per se* such as regularly driving through a red light, driving over the speed limits or taking deadlines up to the wire.[49] This is a low-level version of "extreme" or dangerous sports such as parachuting, white water rafting or hang gliding. There's nothing wrong with the thrill of testing yourself, of course – but if you're driven to take bigger and bigger risks, and they still leave you feeling empty, then you might have a problem.

Relationships

So-called co-dependent relationships have many of the characteristics of an addictive behaviour.[50] Those involved experience low self-esteem, a conflicting need to be both controlling and compliant and, often, the inability to break away from the relationship, even when they know it does not fulfil their needs.

What about behaviours that are harmful in themselves – can they too be addictive?

Behaviours that cause harm to the individual or to others can be addictive – at least in the broadest sense of the term because they can, perversely, afford some pleasure and relief. Self-injury, for instance, is thought to be a coping mechanism which allows relief from tension and stress for some people in much the same way as drinking, smoking or taking drugs does for others.[51] Domestic violence can also be seen as an addiction to the power and thrill of inflicting harm and fear on others; in some individuals, violent activity raises levels of adrenaline, the arousal hormone, creating a "rush" that can be likened to a dopamine "high". Individuals who are prone to violence often show deficits in impulse control which may also be shared by those who are addicted to drugs.

So can ANYTHING be addictive?

No, although as the list of so-called behavioural addictions grows it's easy to believe that it is conceivable for anything to trigger an addiction. Strictly speaking, to be addictive a substance or behaviour activates specific brain circuits – as described above – leading to the experience of reward or pleasure. And there are certain key behaviours and experiences linked to addiction, such as pursuit of the substance or activity, even when it's known to cause harm – as well as tolerance and withdrawal symptoms. So far the list of substances and activities to which these criteria apply is a limited one.

What is the difference between addiction, compulsion and obsession?

Compulsive, driven, behaviour is, as we've seen, an important component of an addiction. Compulsion in itself is a little different; it is an abnormal and uncontrollable need to carry out an action – hand-washing or checking whether switches are turned off are common examples – to gain relief from anxiety. Obsession is an unhealthy preoccupation with an idea – such as how you look, fear of germs, or being in love with someone you don't even know – which may lead to compulsive behaviour focused on that idea. The preoccupation is typically intrusive, repetitive and often makes you feel anxious. People are often aware that their obsessions are irrational, yet they cannot stop the thoughts. Obsession and compulsion can link together in a cycle of behaviour typical of obsessive-compulsive disorder (OCD), where obsessive thoughts drive compulsive behaviour. So an obsession with dirt and germs might lead someone to wash their hands hundreds of times a day, leaving no time for a normal life. While compulsion and preoccupation are characteristic of addictive behaviour and many get relief from anxiety by consuming drugs, addiction and OCD are distinctly different problems (although given the strong co-existence of addiction and mental illness, the same person may suffer from addiction and OCD).

Are you addicted to the internet?

If you already know or strongly believe you are addicted to the internet, this guide will assist you in identifying the areas in your life most impacted by your excessive internet use; and If you're not sure whether you're addicted, this will help determine the answer and begin to assess the damage done. Remember when answering, only consider the time you spent online for non-academic or non-job related purposes.

Answer the following questions awarding the following scores depending on your answer:

1 = rarely

2 = occasionally

3 = frequently

4 = often

5 = always

1. How often do you find that you stay online longer than you intended?
2. How often do you neglect household chores to spend more time online?
3. How often do you prefer the excitement of the internet to intimacy with your partner?
4. How often do you form new relationships with fellow online users?
5. How often do others in your life complain to you about the amount of time you spend online?
6. How often do your grades or school work suffer because of the amount of time you spend online?
7. How often do you check your e-mail before something else that you need to do?

8. How often does your job performance or productivity suffer because of the internet?

9. How often do you become defensive or secretive when anyone asks you what you do online?

10. How often do you block out disturbing thoughts about your life with soothing thoughts of the internet?

11. How often do you find yourself anticipating when you will go online again?

12. How often do you fear that life without the internet would be boring, empty, and joyless?

13. How often do you snap, yell or act annoyed if someone bothers you while you are online?

14. How often do you lose sleep due to late-night log-ins?

15. How often do you feel preoccupied with the internet when offline, or fantasize about being online?

16. How often do you find yourself saying "just a few more minutes" when online?

17. How often do you try to cut down the amount of time you spend online and fail?

18. How often do you try to hide how long you've been online?

19. How often do you choose to spend more time online over going out with others?

20. How often do you feel depressed, moody, or nervous when you are off-line, which goes away once you are back online?

Scores

After you've answered all the questions, add the numbers you selected for each response to obtain a final score. The higher your score, the greater your level of addiction and the problems your internet usage causes.

Here's a general scale to help measure your score:
20–49 points: *you are an average online user. You may surf the web a bit too long at times, but you have control over your usage.*
50–79 points: *you are experiencing occasional or frequent problems because of the internet. You should consider their full impact on your life.*
80–100 points: *your internet usage is causing significant problems in your life. You should evaluate the impact of the internet on your life and address the problems directly caused by your internet usage. After you have identified the category that fits your total score, look back at those questions for which your scored a 4 or 5. Did you realize this was a significant problem for you? For example, if you answered 4 (often) to Question 2 regarding your neglect of household chores, were you aware of just how often your dirty laundry piles up or how empty the refrigerator gets?*

You may have answered 5 (always) to Question 14 about lost sleep due to late-night log-ins. Have you ever stopped to think about how hard it has become to drag yourself out of bed every morning? Do you feel exhausted at work? Has this pattern begun to take its toll on your body and your overall health?

Turn to page 169 for further reading and websites which provide information and advice if you think you may be an internet addict.

6 Recreational drugs

"Why do people use cannabis? They seek a sense of well-being – a relaxed, calm, drowsy, dreamlike state, with a feeling of disconnection from the everyday world."

Dr Avram Goldstein, (Stanford University), *Addiction: From Biology to Drug Policy,* **Oxford University Press, 2001**

Solvent abuse – a young person's problem

Volatile solvents are found in a range of readily available products from lighter fuel to glues and thinners. Glue sniffing, as it's commonly known, is mainly a problem among children and adolescents – with most users aged between 12 and 17 years. Commonly it's a group activity. It is done in two ways – sniffing, which involves inhaling from an open container, and "bagging" , which involves inhalation of vapour from a plastic or paper bag. Inhaling lighter fuel and the contents of a fire extinguisher can be fatal, and any methods involving putting a plastic bag over the head can lead to asphyxiation.

The high from solvent abuse – including euphoria and exhilaration – occurs rapidly and is similar to being drunk. But the impact dissipates so rapidly that parents and teachers may not be aware that a young person is using solvents. The various health effects include lung and gastrointestinal symptoms and, more seriously, shortness of breath and palpitations.

Solvents have a sedating effect on the central nervous system and young people who use solvents are at risk of accidents when under the influence. Some users just experiment as part of adolescent rebellion; but for others it may be part of a more widespread pattern of risk behaviour.

Criteria for substance dependence in ICD-10 (International Statistical Classification of Diseases)

Addiction of various kinds is normally diagnosed with the following standard questionnaire. Three or more of the following must have been experienced or exhibited together at some time during the previous year.

1. A strong desire/compulsion to take the substance.
2. Difficulties in controlling substance-taking behaviour.
3. Withdrawal symptoms if substance use stops or is reduced and perhaps attempts to reduce discomfort by returning to use of the original or a related substance.
4. Evidence of tolerance, so increased doses are needed to get the original effect.
5. Neglect of alternative pleasures or interests because of substance use.
6. Increased amount of time necessary to obtain or take the substance or to recover from its effects.
7. Persisting with substance use despite clear evidence of harmful consequences, such as harm to the liver through excessive drinking, depressed mood after binges, and social or personal problems. Efforts should be made to determine that the user was actually, or could be expected to be, aware of the nature and extent of the harm.

Source: World Health Organization

What are the effects of cannabis?

Cannabis comes from the plant *Cannabis sativa*. Herbal cannabis (also known as grass, ganga or marijuana) comes from the leaves and stem of the plant and looks like dry tobacco. Cannabis resin (hash, hashish) is scraped or rubbed from the plant and is usually pressed into small blocks that look like stock cubes. The drug is either smoked as a hand-rolled cigarette (joint, spliff) or the resin can be baked in cakes or added to drinks. Smoked cannabis takes effect within minutes but only stays in the body for an hour or so. When eaten or drunk, the drug takes about an hour to work but the effects may last 12 hours or longer.

The active ingredients of cannabis are compounds called cannabinoids, such as tetrahydrocannibol (THC). Like alcohol, cannabis acts on the brain as a depressant by binding to molecules called cannabinoid receptors. It tends to produce a feeling of mild relaxation, sometimes even euphoria and a sense of "distance" from surrounding objects. Some people find it makes them more talkative, while others become introspective under its influence.

The downside is that high doses of cannabis can produce panic, paranoia and hallucinations. However, it does not produce any of the short- or long-term adverse effects that are associated with alcohol, such as slurring of speech, lack of co-ordination, hangover or long-term liver damage. Research has shown no serious toxic effects associated with THC. One side-effect of taking cannabis, however, is a powerful urge to eat. Research on mice show that natural derivatives of cannabis in the brain – endocannabinoids – that bind to the same receptors play an important role in appetite.

Cannabis can certainly cause psychological dependence, with regular users finding it hard to give up in the same manner as tobacco smokers. Whether cannabis is really a "gateway" to harder drugs like cocaine remains debatable.

An experience of LSD

 I bought a small tablet. We all went out for a meal and I had forgotten I had taken the tablet. I had ordered a pancake that began looking like an ice cream sundae, rather like a piece of sculpture, the visual captivity of which invited touching and handling. My hands waved over the top, making conjuror's passes at it. We wandered back to someone's flat, put some records on and the walls of the room started breathing, which gave me a nice, warm comfortable feeling. People were drifting in and out and, at one point, I thought I would like to look at the stars but felt it was safer inside. Various pictures came alive and started to talk to me. One was of Bob Dylan. Those things that were real in the first place became more real and I felt that I was going through a whole dream state. Surrealist paintings are not far off it – there was a point of increasing religious experience, a sense of something very much greater, something up and above, very warm, light, bright, becoming something inside that I would have thought was a soul or a mind trying to blossom and extend from it. I was getting what I found to be overload on some video cameras. Most of the experiences I had were exaggerations of what was already there.

Music that contained scratches put me in mind of a lovely log fire. Then I was in a tropical place and I was experiencing ME from a very young age to adulthood – all at the same time. I knew it was interesting, I don't know if I learned anything from it, but it was important to me to see myself simultaneously during all these years. By now it was getting towards the end of the trip. Now that I am reliving this, it seems to me that it was tremendously inward looking. Another person, who was not having a good trip, came in, tore up their cheque book and went out again. The whole of my trip was in brilliant colour. There was one slightly bad moment when I was coming out of it. I looked in the mirror and saw a slight cut above my eye. I told myself that this was interesting but it is only a trick. The whole thing took about twelve hours. It was like taking a look at reality in a three dimensional way. For weeks afterwards, I was aware that whatever I saw, there was always a little bit more around it.

"Jules", from *Streetwise, Drugwise,* Eva Roman, Richard James, Management Books 2000, 1998

Therapeutic cannabis

Today nabilone, a synthetic cannabinoid, and THC (Marinol) are used in some countries to relieve the nausea that accompanies chemotherapy for cancer. Personal accounts of the benefits of cannabis in relieving pain and other symptoms in multiple sclerosis (MS) are also widespread. However, in 1973, the medical use of cannabis was banned in the United Kingdom under the Misuse of Drugs Act because it was generally believed to have no therapeutic benefit. Recent years have seen a change of opinion; up to four per cent of the MS patients in the UK are now reported to turn to cannabis for symptom relief. They'll continue to be criminalized for this, however, unless the mass of anecdotal evidence on cannabis – that it helps with neuropathic pain (caused by nerve damage), stimulates appetite and reduces nausea – is turned into hard scientific fact.

So far, around 1,000 patients have taken part in trials that have demonstrated the benefits of cannabis as an oral spray containing THC and CBD (cannabidiol) for pain, spasticity (muscle stiffness and spasms) and other symptoms in multiple sclerosis and other neurological conditions. Trials of medical cannabis for cancer pain and spinal cord injury are also underway. Other potential applications are in rheumatoid arthritis and psychotic disorders.

Meanwhile, the Medical Research Council and the Multiple Sclerosis Society have reported in the medical journal *The Lancet* on the largest ever trial of cannabis and MS, involving over 600 patients. In the Cannabinoids in MS Trial (CAMS), patients received either whole cannabis extract, synthetic THC, or a placebo for 15 weeks. Although an objective measure of spasticity showed no difference between the groups, a majority of those on cannabis did perceive an improvement in spasticity, pain and sleep quality. MS is a complex condition and more attention needs to be paid to each patient's experience. Mobility, as measured by time to walk a fixed distance, was also increased in the cannabis groups.

The pleasures of Ecstasy

MDMA has become known as as a "dance drug" because it increases energy, stamina and sociability. However if people dance through the night, the adverse effects of the drug can be exacerbated – dehydration, high body temperature and potentially, convulsions and kidney failure. It's important to drink plenty of water after taking Ecstasy for these reasons. A further complication can be that even water can be toxic – even fatal – if you consume too much, as it can can cause swelling of the brain. Although tolerance to the effects of Ecstasy has been noted – more of the drug is needed to get the same effect if you use it a lot – unlike heroin, stopping it does not cause withdrawal symptoms. It appears to have less potential for addiction as it does not seem to be used compulsively on a long-term basis.

Why is heroin so dangerous?

Long-term heroin dependence is the most common reason for addicts in the UK to request treatment. Heroin (diamorphine) is one of a group of drugs which include compounds such as heroin derived from the opium poppy (known as opiates) and synthetic derivatives (which are sometimes also known as opioids). They have a number of medical uses, chiefly for relieving severe pain. Heroin is taken either by sniffing, smoking ("chasing the dragon") or by injection.

   Heroin and other opiates have a wide range of effects – euphoria, analgesia, sedation and depression of the respiratory system. Intravenous injection leads to euphoria – best described as an intense feeling of wellbeing and sometimes called a "rush" . Research shows that opiates bind to specialized opioid receptors throughout the brain. In the ventral tegmental area, when heroin binds to opioid receptors, it inhibits the action of neurons that would otherwise block the production of dopamine – this increases dopamine transmission in the mesolimbic dopamine system. Tolerance to heroin develops rapidly as exposure produces desensitization of the opioid receptors so more is needed to get the same effect.

It is the factors associated with heroin addiction that cause the most damage. For instance, tolerance fades when someone stops using the drug. If they then relapse – a common occurrence because of the long-term brain changes that develop with chronic use – they may overdose on a dose that they could easily cope with before. Overdose can be fatal, as it interferes with the breathing centre of the brain, causing respiratory depression.

Over time and with regular use, more heroin is needed to get the same effect. It is also expensive (weight for weight, it's more expensive than gold) so users often get into financial difficulties and may turn to crime to fund their habit. Withdrawal, while not life-threatening, can be very unpleasant and this deters many users from even trying to give up.

Intravenous injection of heroin achieves the most intense experience for a given dose, but when performed under non-sterile conditions (sharing injecting equipment, for example) it can lead to the transmission of HIV and the hepatitis C virus. Finally, the purity and potency of street heroin is usually unknown, so usage carries the risk of overdose (which may be fatal) as well as other serious health risks. Unsurprisingly, the death rate for heroin addicts may be up to 50 times higher than for non-addicts of the same age.

An experience with heroin

 The first time I tried it, it made me really sick. To begin with, I smoked it – I didn't inject for quite a long time, and then the sensation was really amazing. It was not the same as LSD; it was really warm and comfortable, no nervous anxiety. You feel as if your body is a shell and everything inside is hollow. It is not hallucinogenic, and you can increase or decrease the dose as you want. The first thing I found out about heroin was that in cold weather you don't have to switch on electricity since it makes you feel nice and warm.

"Lindsay", from *Streetwise, Drugwise,* Eva Roman, Richard James, Management Books 2000, 1998

Part Two
Treatment for addiction

1 Treating addiction

"In many ways, the substance abuse treatment field is where the schizophrenia field was 50 years ago. The understanding of alcoholism and addiction as diseases of the brain is rapidly gaining great acceptance."

Dr Richard Rawson, (University of California, Los Angeles), *Journal of Psychoactive Drugs,* **2000**

What medical treatments are available for addiction?

A better understanding of how drugs work on the brain is beginning to change views about treatment for addiction. As in the treatment of other disorders – for example, heart disease, cancer and infection – medication has its part to play. There are already drugs that can help to treat nicotine, opiate and alcohol addiction. Meanwhile, researchers are still searching for effective medical treatments for addiction to stimulants such as cocaine and amphetamines.

Clinical trials and expert opinion have suggested that drug treatment for addiction works best in conjunction with some form of psychological therapy. For instance, there is no conflict between the use of the drug naltrexone to treat alcohol addiction and the "12 Steps" programme used by Alcoholics Anonymous[52] (see page 141). Nicotine replacement therapy, to help wean people off cigarettes, has more chance of success if the individual is also offered counselling.

A two-fold approach is often necessary because addiction is a multi-faceted problem. Failure to address any pre-existing mental health, social and domestic problems – that may, or may not, be related to drug use – will greatly decrease the chances of successful treatment. Drug and behavioural habits become deeply ingrained and radical change is needed to fill the void left by giving up.

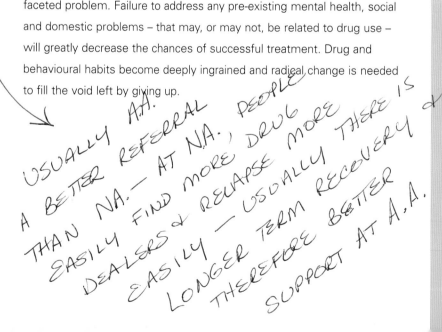

USUALLY A.A. A BETTER REFERRAL THAN N.A. – AT N.A., PEOPLE EASILY FIND MORE DRUG DEALERS & RELAPSE MORE EASILY – USUALLY THERE IS LONGER TERM RECOVERY & THEREFORE BETTER SUPPORT AT A.A.

What's involved in treatment for addiction?

Treatment of drug addiction falls into two main phases. First, support is needed through the detoxification process, during which exposure to the drug is reduced and then withdrawn. Benzodiazepine tranquillizers, for example, can alleviate some of the symptoms of alcohol withdrawal. Once the withdrawal process is complete, however, the chances of relapse are very high and other drugs, such as methadone and buprenorphine, both of which are used to treat opiate addiction, may be prescribed. In heroin addiction, these drugs provide a substitute for the action of heroin in the brain. Both are agonists at the opioid receptors but they do not produce the same "rush" as heroin. As both are taken orally, they also do not have the health risks associated with heroin injection. It can, however, take a very long time to withdraw from methadone and some heroin addicts remain on it indefinitely.

Nicotine replacement therapy for smoking works in a similar way – by providing the nicotine in gradually reduced doses, but not the harmful tar or smoke. The aim is to eventually withdraw from the substitutes altogether.

The second, and probably more difficult, phase involves keeping free of the drug and preventing relapse, which is where the psychological therapies play a really important role.

Drugs used in treating addiction in the UK

(excluding antidepressants and nicotine replacement therapy)

Drug name [Brand name]	Therapeutic use
Acamprosate [Campral]	Maintenance of abstinence in alcohol-dependent patients; should be used with counselling
Buprenorphine [Subutex]	Substitution treatment for opiate drug dependence; should be used in a framework of medical, social and psychological treatment
Bupropion [Zyban]	Smoking cessation for nicotine-dependent patients; best used with motivational support
Lofexidine [BritLofex]	Relief of withdrawal symptoms in patients undergoing opiate detoxification
Methadone	Substitution treatment of opiate drug addiction
Naloxone	Treatment of respiratory depression in opiate drug overdose
Naltrexone [Nalorex]	Prophylactic therapy in maintenance of detoxified, formerly opiate-dependent patients

Information from www.emc.medicines.org.uk (Electronic Medicines Compendium)

NOTE: COMPLETE ABSTINENCE FROM NARCOTICS, BENZO's & ALCOHOL WILL BE ESSENTIAL.

How I gave up smoking

Until recently, I'd never seriously thought about stopping, mainly because smoking didn't appear to be affecting my health. During my two pregnancies, I found it quite easy to stay off cigarettes, but a couple of days after the births, I was smoking again. It was only in the last couple of years that I started to think seriously about stopping. Several things had got me thinking. My father died just before my youngest daughter, Ashleigh, was born. He was a sixty-a-day, whisky-drinking, "let's-eat-lots-of-pies" type of person. He had three heart attacks, and then the fourth finally got him. If he'd knocked smoking on the head, I think he could have had another few years. Then three years ago, I had a nasty dose of pneumonia, but the thing that really clinched it was turning 40!

I went to my doctor for some advice. He put me in touch with a counsellor at a smoking cessation service, and I arranged a quit date with her. I decided to stop on September 5th, the day the girls went back to school. The night I finally quit, it was easy for me: I had my patches ready, my little emergency bag of tricks and the counsellor's phone number to hand.

The first few days were difficult, and I tried to ignore the cravings as much as possible. Paul (my husband) was a great help. I'd say, "God! I really want a cigarette," and he'd say, "Quick, have a cup of tea!" I kept distracting myself by picking up a book or a magazine. I used 24-hour patches to get myself through the most difficult stages. My counsellor advised me to get some nicotine gum too, because the nicotine from the patch takes a few hours to kick in, whereas the gum has an almost instant effect.

I used to think smoking relaxed me, but surprisingly I'm more chilled out as a non-smoker! It's only been six weeks since I quit, but I feel brilliant! I can run further now without getting out of breath and I look so much better. I have put on a few pounds, but once I've got over the first couple of months, then I'll concentrate on getting back in shape. My husband bought me my first ever bike for my birthday, so I'll be going out cycling with the girls and hopefully lose the extra weight that way! I've also been putting some money away every week and I've saved about £120 so far. I'll probably splash out on either a new fitted kitchen or a dishwasher. That'll be my treat!

Bar manager and mum of two, Louise McIlhone, from ASH website, formerly published in STOP magazine

What is detoxing?

Detoxing or detoxification literally means ridding the body of toxins which have accumulated through drug dependence. It involves stopping the drug of abuse and dealing with any withdrawal symptoms. Detoxing is important – it is the first step on the road to freedom from an addiction. Some treatment programmes won't accept addicts unless they have first gone through some form of detoxing.

The detoxing process can be undertaken in many ways – rapidly or gradually, with or without drugs (to help with the discomfort of withdrawal symptoms), and on an in-patient or out-patient basis. Some heroin addicts, for instance, choose to just stop their drug – going "cold turkey" – and rely on the support of others in a residential setting to help them get through the experience.

Detoxing is different for each drug because, just as each drug has a different effect on the brain, so too does withdrawal. Long-term drug use, as we've seen, causes permanent alterations in brain chemistry and architecture which often mean the person is literally dependent on the drug to keep the brain in a stable state. Removal of the drug from the receptors in the brain causes a rebound effect – withdrawal – characterized by each drug. It is worth mentioning again that, generally speaking, a combination of medical and psychological treatment works best for the long-term maintenance treatment of most people.

The effects of withdrawal

Heroin. Withdrawal from heroin and other opiates produces a characteristic range of withdrawal symptoms including nausea, vomiting and diarrhoea, stomach cramps, aches and pains, chills, racing heart, yawning, runny eyes and insomnia. These symptoms arise from the sudden excitability of noradrenaline neurons in an area of the brain called the locus coeruleus, when heroin molecules cease to occupy receptors within these neurons.[53] Although withdrawal from heroin involves profound discomfort – it has been described as similar to a severe case of flu – it is not regarded as medically serious and is almost never life-threatening. The effects are over within seven to ten days, with the symptoms peaking between 24 and 72 hours after stopping heroin – even for those who've been on very high doses. Heroin withdrawal can be managed without medication, but many addicts seem to dread the prospect of withdrawal and it may deter some from coming forward for treatment. It therefore makes sense to do everything possible to ease the discomfort. Gradually decreasing doses of methadone given over 10 to 28 days have been found to be effective in treating heroin withdrawal.[54] Clonidine and lofexidine are drugs that can stop the excessive firing of the neurons in the locus coeruleus and have been shown to ease the pain of withdrawal.[55]

Benzodiazepines. The benzodiazepine tranquillizers, such as diazepam and temezepam, are widely used by many opiate addicts. Once widely prescribed for even mild anxiety, tranquillizers produced severe dependence in many who used no other drugs. Withdrawal may produce only mild symptoms of anxiety, apprehension and insomnia that need no treatment other than reassurance. Others have reported more severe problems, such as hallucinations, depersonalization, paranoia and even seizures. Benzodiazepine withdrawal symptoms can be treated by a gradually tapering dose of a long-acting barbiturate (phenobarbitone), or a long-acting benzodiazepine (chlordiazepoxide).

Alcohol. Withdrawal from alcohol can be very unpleasant – even life-threatening. Shakiness is common (especially among chronic drinkers in the morning before the first drink of the day) and may be accompanied by restlessness, agitation and insomnia. Sounds such as buzzing and ringing in the ears and even auditory hallucinations, may occur. The most severe form of withdrawal is delirium tremens (DTs). DTs may cause extreme feelings of agitation, restlessness, confusion and hallucinations as well as even death from accidents, dehydration, hypothermia or pneumonia, and so needs urgent medical attention. Alcohol withdrawal can be managed with benzodiazepines such as chlordiazepoxide and, where symptoms are very severe, lorazepam or diazepam may be given by injection.

Many people believe that detoxification is all that's needed to withdraw from a drug habit. But detox alone rarely produces long-term abstinence – it is just the first stage of a long-term process. Detox is necessary, but not sufficient, to become free of an addiction.

Always consult your doctor before initially undertaking, changing or stopping of drug treatment for addiction.

Arsenal v. Liverpool 25.10.89

 I remember the game for conventional reasons, for Smith's late winner as substitute and thus a handy Cup win over the old enemy. But most of all I remember it as the only time in the 1980s and, hitherto, the 1990s, that I had no nicotine in my bloodstream for the entire ninety minutes. I have gone through games without smoking in that time: during the first half of the 83/84 season I was on nicotine chewing gum, but never managed to kick that, and in the end went back to the cigarettes. But in October 1989, after a visit to Allen Carr the anti-smoking guru, I went cold turkey for ten days, and this game came right in the middle of that unhappy period.

I want to stop smoking and, like many people who wish to do the same, I firmly believe that abstinence is just around the corner. I won't buy a carton of duty-frees, or a lighter, or even a household-sized box of matches because, given the imminence of my cessation, it would be a waste of money. What stops me from doing so now, today, this minute, are the things that have always stopped me: a difficult period of work up ahead, requiring the kind of concentration that only a Silk Cut can facilitate; the fear of the overwhelming domestic tension that would doubtless accompany screaming desperation; and, inevitably and pathetically, the Arsenal.

They do give me some leeway. There's the first half of the season, before the FA Cup begins, and before the Championship has warmed up. And there are times like now, when with my team out of everything by the end of January I am looking at almost five months of dull but tension-free afternoons. (But I've got this book to write, and deadlines, and...). And yet some seasons – the 88/89 Championship year, for example, or the chase for the Double in 90/91, where every game between January and May was crucial – I cannot contemplate what it would be like to sit there without a smoke. Two down against Tottenham in a Cup semi-final at Wembley with eleven minutes gone and no fag? Inconceivable.

From *Fever Pitch*, Nick Hornby, Penguin Books, 1992

Heroin withdrawal: are there any medications that can make opiate detoxification easier?

Clonidine and lofexidine are both drugs called alpha-2-adrenergic agonists, the role of which is to lower the firing of noradrenergic neurons and noradrenaline turnover. One of their effects is to lower blood pressure and another is to dampen down the symptoms of opiate withdrawal. Clonidine and lofexidine were orginally designed to treat high blood pressure, but lofexidine, the newer of the two drugs, is less effective in this context. However, an analysis of the evidence shows that lofexidine may be a more useful drug than clonidine when it comes to opiate detoxification.[56] The blood-pressure-lowering effect of clonidine causes problems for some and means that it can only be taken under close medical supervision. Lofexidine is not effective in lowering blood pressure and comparisons of the two show that lofexidine does not cause the same problem of hypotension. This means it can be used more widely. Both drugs are equally effective in reducing withdrawal symptoms – within about five days, which is faster than with methadone. Because it is effective and has fewer side-effects, lofexidine has been used increasingly in detox regimes in recent years. It may be particularly useful in contexts where methadone abuse might be an issue (for example in prisons) and more acceptable to clinicians who aren't happy with prescribing methadone.

What is rapid detox?

It is possible to break heroin addiction in a short period of time using a method known as 'rapid detox'. The method is based on the observation that giving large doses of the opiate antagonists naltrexone or naloxone will trigger acute withdrawal from heroin; this could be complete in as little as two days. Symptoms can be relieved by the administration of sedatives, such as benzodiazepines or by clonidine, a drug that reduces noradrenergic (noradrenaline) activity in the central nervous system. From here it is, perhaps a logical step, to start using general anaesthesia as a "cover" for withdrawal symptoms induced by opiate antagonists. In fact, sleep or coma therapy has a long history in the treatment of mental illness – insulin coma was once used for schizophrenia, while deep sleep therapy was used for morphine dependence.

Opiate antagonist treatment under general anaesthesia is known as ultrarapid opiate detoxification (rapid detox) and, in the last 15 years or so, it has been widely used, especially in private clinics. However, the method remains controversial.[57] On the one hand, the prospect of a rapid and relatively painless treatment may attract people whose fear of the detoxification process keeps them away from treatment. The short "down time" of 24 hours or so appeals to those who are willing to take a tough stance. There is also the argument that addicts should be entitled to the same pain relief as those suffering from other problems. After all, it is expected that anaesthesia will be offered during tooth extraction or childbirth. However, general anaesthesia always carries a risk to health – albeit a very small one. Many people with addictions may have other medical problems, such as liver disease, which make a general anaesthetic especially risky. The patient generally receives a "cocktail" of drugs while under anaesthesia, which may raise safety issues.

There have not been many large scale clinical trials of rapid detox – a cause for concern given how widely available the procedure now seems to be. There is a danger that the speed and simplicity of rapid detox may make the addicted individual forget that he or she has a long-term problem. There is not much data on the rates of long-term abstinence after rapid detox. As with all other treatments, motivation, support and some form of therapy are probably essential for the best chance of success. A recent review of rapid detox has concluded that expert support can minimize the potential dangers,[58] making this a viable option for the treatment of heroin abuse.

How does methadone work?

Methadone is an opioid-receptor antagonist, first synthesized by German chemists as a substitute for morphine in World War II. It has been used as a treatment for opiate dependence since the 1960s following work by Professor Vincent Dole and his team at Rockefeller University in the US who were among the first to believe that addiction is a brain disorder. Today, most countries that have a problem with heroin addiction also run methadone treatment programmes – making methadone the most thoroughly-investigated of all the addiction treatments.[59]

Methadone acts on the same sites in the brain as heroin but does not produce any euphoria or sedation. It has a long half life – 24 hours – so it only needs to be administered once a day. Steady blood levels of a drug are more satisfying to the addict than the peaks and troughs of methadone, so it therefore does not give the same pleasurable sensation as heroin. Methadone helps prevent heroin withdrawal symptoms and also reduces cravings by blocking the receptor sites that heroin would occupy in the brain. It is available as a tablet or as an injection. The latter is meant only for those who fail to respond to oral methadone. It also introduces the addict to a clinical setting where other help can be given.

Is methadone treatment actually effective?

There is considerable variation in how methadone is used – both between and within countries – regarding dose, formulation, extent of supervision, and other treatments and services that might be offered along with the medication. Many programmes around the world – both public and private – have the aim of harm reduction rather than abstinence – that is, reducing the risks of HIV or other infections by substituting an oral drug for an injectable one or reducing criminal, drug-seeking behaviour. Such programmes maintain the addict on methadone for long periods or even indefinitely (methadone maintenance treatment). However, methadone treatment can also be used in a tapering fashion (methadone reduction treatment). While it is not yet clear which treatment works better, research has shown that whatever the context, methadone is effective. According to a recent study, 59 per cent of addicts showed a reduction in the use of illicit drugs, although 22 per cent showed little or no improvement.[60]

A broad analysis of methadone maintenance treatment shows that the goals of harm reduction are at least partly met, with a decrease in the use of illicit opiates, a reduction in HIV risk taking and reductions in criminal behaviour.[61]

To get the most out of methadone, it is best to combine it with other help in a treatment setting – from counselling and HIV testing to primary health care and psychiatric assessment. One study has compared methadone alone to methadone plus counselling to methadone plus "enhanced" psychosocial support (consisting of counselling with extended medical/psychiatric, employment and family therapy services) – the highest level of support.[62] The latter investment was well worthwhile with those involved showing improvements in employment status, decreases in drug use and illegal activity, better relationships and better mental health, compared to those receiving methadone alone or methadone plus standard counselling. Some of those receiving methadone alone showed improvements, but 41 per cent had to be transferred onto the standard programme (i.e. with counselling) for their own protection, because of continued drug use and medical or psychiatric emergencies. This study underlines the complexity of treatment of drug addiction – it is unlikely there will ever be a "magic bullet" that can normalize the brain systems that have been damaged by drug use. Psychosocial treatments will always need to go hand in hand with medication.

Are there any other treatments for heroin addiction?

Despite its proven effectiveness, methadone remains an imperfect treatment that does not bring benefit to all those who try it. Methadone is controversial – its critics (those who advocate abstinence as the only way to deal with addiction) say that it merely substitutes a legal opioid for an illegal opiate. Methadone will continue to play an important role in the treatment of opiate addiction for the foreseeable future. There are also other drugs, though, such as buprenorphine and the opioid antagonists naloxone and naltrexone, that are being used increasingly in the treatment of heroin addiction.

SEE PRESCRIPTION FOR NUTRITIONAL HEALING by BALCH

Natural recovery from heroin addiction

Researchers in London followed up a group of 128 individuals who were being prescribed heroin at drug clinics around the capital between 1969 and 1979 [63]. This study showed that the addicts were a diverse group with the typical "junkie" (see page 26) being in the minority (18 of the group). By 1975, 40 per cent of the group were no longer attending the clinics. What had happened to them? Had they given up heroin? Remarkably, the researchers managed to track down 97 per cent of the original group and interviewed most of them, making it the longest and most comprehensive ever follow-up of a group of heroin addicts.

Eleven men and four women had died, at an average age of 30, and all were still dependent on drugs at the time of their death. The death rate was much higher than for the average population of this age. Five people were in prison (but abstinent). Sixty-two people were still on opiates, most of them still in contact with the clinic. However, some of them were living stable lives in the community. Forty people were no longer using heroin and were also living in the community. Nine of these were still using psychoactive drugs, but their pattern of use was no different from that of the average person.

This does seem like a remarkably good success rate for natural recovery. As you might expect, those who had stopped using heroin were now living different lives – not in touch with former drug-using friends, in stable employment, in good health and with few obvious problems. Taken overall, this study gives an optimistic message – many people do have the power within themselves to heal an addiction.

SMALL 6 MEALS/DAY RECOMMENDED IN ALL CASES TO KEEP BLOOD SUGAR LEVELS STEADY & THEREFORE PREVENT CRAVINGS OR MINIMIZE

"DON'T GET TOO HUNGRY, ANGRY, LONELY OR TIRED" IS A GOOD REMINDER — AA'S OLD SAYING

What are the advantages of buprenorphine treatment?

Buprenorphine has been used worldwide as an analgesic (drug that relieves pain) for several decades, but has only recently been applied as a treatment for opiate addiction. It is in a different class from methadone and heroin, being a partial not a full agonist at the brain receptors that register heroin stimulation. It therefore activates the receptor in a very limited way. If a partial agonist is given to someone who is not opiate dependent, it has the full stimulant effect, but if it is given to someone who is opiate dependent, it's partial effect may even precipitate withdrawal.

It is thought that as there is a "ceiling" on the effects of buprenorphine, it is less likely to produce breathing or heart-rate difficulties and is therefore safer. It has been used in France since 1996. The drug is usually taken under the tongue, so it can be absorbed into the body through the mucous membranes of the mouth.

In a comparison study, 220 heroin addicts were assigned to methadone (low or high dose), buprenorphine or LAAM.[64] (Note that LAAM – leva-alpha acetyl methadol – has been now been withdrawn because of toxicity.) This showed that buprenorphine was as effective as LAAM or high-dose methadone, with those treated reporting major reductions in heroin use. Moreover, the drug's mixed action on the brain's receptors may lead to less severe withdrawal symptoms than with heroin or methadone. A study from Sweden has shown that the combination of buprenorphine and psychosocial support gives good results.[65] The trial covered 40 heroin addicts who received either buprenorphine or placebo with cognitive behaviour group therapy aimed at reducing relapse. They all had weekly individual counselling and three times weekly urine analysis to detect illicit drug use. At the end of the year, 75 per cent of those in the buprenorphine group remained in the programme compared to none in the placebo group (again demonstrating the relative ineffectiveness of just one treatment approach). Of those still in the programme, urine screens were 75 per cent negative for illicit drugs, showing that the buprenorphine/cognitive therapy approach is remarkably effective.

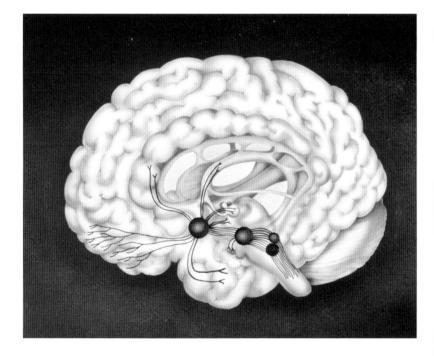

Artwork of the human brain featuring the binding sites and pathways (in red) of opiate (morphine- type) drugs. The mechanisms of pain perception and analgesia, the action of pain-killing drugs on the brain, have received intensive biochemical study. In the brainstem (rightmost two red spheres), sites involved in the transmission of pain include the nucleus raphe magnus and locus coeruleus, with other nuclei in the hypothalamus and thalamus (circles to the left). Nerve pathways (red) extend to the frontal cortex (far left) and up into the limbic system (centre-left). Sites involved in altering reactivity to pain are less well identified.

The role of antidepressants

Antidepressants are psychoactive drugs too and, because they are prescription medications, the way they act on the brain to improve mood has been intensively studied. A discussion is relevant here because the study of antidepressant action can help us understand the brain better. In most cases, antidepressants are not addictive, despite popular belief. Sometimes, as we'll see in the next chapter, they can be useful in the treatment of addiction, especially when depression is also present.

Around 70 per cent of patients treated for depression with an antidepressant will see an improvement within three months. The newer drugs, such as the selective serotonin reuptake inhibitors (SSRIs), don't seem to be much more effective than older drugs but are often preferred because they have fewer side effects. All antidepressants work by altering brain chemistry, mainly to increase serotonin and noradrenaline within the synapses. However, we don't know that depression is actually *caused* by lower levels of these neurotransmitters. While the effects of antidepressants on brain chemistry start almost immediately, the patient doesn't usually feel any relief until they have been on medication for a few weeks, even though side effects are experienced much sooner. Newer antidepressants have a shorter "time lag" to action. The main types of antidepressant raise serotonin and/or noradrenaline mechanisms in different ways which, as we have seen, can be related to addictive behaviour:

■ Tricyclic antidepressants (e.g. imipramine [Tofranil], nortriptyline [Allegron, Motival]), increase neurotransmitter levels in the brain. Tricyclics are one of the older types of antidepressants. They work by preventing noradrenaline and serotonin from being sucked back up from the synaptic gap before they can attach to the target (post-synaptic) cell and stimulate it into action. They also affect circuits in the brain that use another neurotransmitter, acetylcholine. This can cause a number of unpleasant side-effects, including

Giving up heroin

 I can tell you that prison is child's play compared with rehab – it is really hard work. My heroin addiction was taken completely out of my hands once I got to the centre. I got no help in the reduction; it was cold turkey all the way. It took about ten days to cross the pain barrier and you walked around with what was like a bad case of 'flu all the time. It was all played down and we were discouraged from moaning and groaning since we were all in the same boat. It took me months to re-establish a natural sleep pattern again and I spent many a night sitting on the top step of the staircase stroking the cat.

"Lindsay", in _Streetwise, Drugwise_, Eva Roman, Richard James, Management Books, 1998

dry mouth, weight gain, dizziness, blurred vision and constipation. An overdose may be fatal.

- Monoamine oxidase inhibitors (e.g. tranylcypromine [parnate]) block the action of an enzyme called monoamine oxidase (MAO), which breaks down noradrenaline, serotonin and dopamine. They are dangerous taken with certain types of food and drink such as cheese, red wine and yeast extract. These products contain high concentrations of a drug called tyramine, which is normally broken down by MAO in the liver. If the enzyme is blocked by the antidepressant, tyramine enters the bloodstream and may caused a sudden, potentially dangerous rise in blood pressure. A newer type of MAOI, moclobemide (Manerix), "reverses" the blocking action if tyramine builds up too high, but does not work for everyone who has benefited from the older type of drugs.

- Selective serotonin reuptake inhibitors (e.g. fluoxetine [Prozac], citalopram [Cipramil]). These "designer" drugs are more specific than the older generation of tablets. They work by blocking reuptake of serotonin only, not noradrenaline. They have fewer side effects than the drugs above and are safer in overdose, but they may still cause sexual dysfunction and nausea.

- Selective noradrenaline reuptake inhibitors e.g. reboxetine [Edronax]. Again, these are more specific in the way they act on brain chemistry. They block only noradrenaline re-uptake, not affecting serotonin. These drugs seem to tackle aspects of depression such as social withdrawal.

- Noradrenaline and selective serotonin reuptake inhibitors (e.g. mirtazapine [Zispin]). The latest generation of antidepressant, these block noradrenaline autoreceptors on pre-synaptic neurons. These are receptors that sense levels of neurotransmitter within the synapse. If levels are high enough, further synthesis is blocked – a form of negative feedback. Blocking the receptor allows synthesis to continue and so raises levels. Mirtazapine also blocks two serotonin receptor subtypes called 5-HT$_2$ and 5-HT$_3$ so that serotonin only reacts with the 5-HT$_1$ subtype. Side effects are linked to serotonin binding to the former two receptor subtypes, so mirtazapine is a very "clean" drug.

Do antidepressants help in the treatment of addiction?

While the links between addictive behaviour and depression are not entirely understood, the use of antidepressant medication for the treatment of depression is, of course, well-established and several new drugs, such as reboxetine and mirtazapine, have been introduced in recent years. Generally, these have fewer side effects than the older antidepressants and are now being prescribed more widely. Specific examples of the use of antidepressants in the treatment of addiction are mentioned (SSRIs for shopping addiction, page 131, bupropion for smoking cessation, page 121).

Antidepressants may play a useful role in the treatment of substance misuse. For instance, there is a strong link between heavy smoking and depression. Smokers are twice as likely as the rest of the population to have depression; and smokers who are depressed are half as likely to be able to give up, compared to those who are not depressed.[66] Besides the antidepressant bupropion, fluoxetine, doxepin [Sinequan] and moclobemide have been shown to alleviate withdrawal symptoms and, in tests, patients had higher abstinence rates than those on placebo (though relapse rates were high).[67] Another drug that might be prescribed for smoking cessation is the tricyclic antidepressant nortriptyline which seems to have a similar success rate to bupropion, though few clinical trials have been done to confirm this.

Cocaine users are three times more likely than average to suffer from depression.[68] Some trials have also shown that antidepressants may reduce cocaine use.[69] However, there are potentially dangerous interactions between antidepressants and stimulants, for instance, monoamine oxidase inhibitors can cause a dramatic increase in blood pressure and bupropion lowers the threshold for seizure. SSRIs may be a safer option.

Antidepressants listed by drug

Drug type	Name of drug [Brand name]
Tricyclic antidepressant (TCA)	Imipramine [Tofranil], nortriptyline [Allegron], amitriptyline, dothiepin [Prothiaden], lofepramine [Gamanil], clomipramine [Anafranil]
Tetracyclic antidepressants	Amoxapine [Asendis], maprotiline [Ludiomil]
Monoamine oxidase inhibitor (MAOI)	Moclobemide [Manerix]
Selective serotonin reuptake inhibitor (SSRI)	Fluoxetine [Prozac], citalopram [Cipramil], paroxetine [Seroxat], fluvoxamine [Faverin], sertraline [Lustral]
Selective noradrenaline reuptake inhibitor (NARI)	Reboxetine [Edronax]
Noradrenaline and selective serotonin antidepressant (NaSSA)	Mirtazapine [Zispin]
Atypical antidepressant (generally have some SSRI and some TCA, or other, character)	venlafaxine [Efexor], trazodone [Molipaxin]

Information from http://emc.medicines.org.uk/ (Electronic Medicines Compendium)

Does all of this mean that drug addiction is a sign of depression?

There is a strong relationship between alcohol and depression. Around half of those who are alcohol dependent have some degree of depression. [70] It is still not clear whether depression drives people to drink, or vice versa, but while alcohol makes you feel relaxed and uninhibited, its overall impact – especially with heavy, regular intake – is to make you feel more depressed. If you are feeling low, it is best to try to avoid alcohol as it will probably make you feel worse. Various studies have shown that antidepressants such as imipramine and fluoxetine reduce relapse when compared to placebo. [71]

Depression is reflected in an alteration in brain chemistry, such as lower levels of serotonin and dopamine. There is also evidence of dysregulation in the mesolimbic dopamine system which may make it harder for depressed people to feel pleasure. [72] However, not all people with a drug problem are depressed. Nevertheless, antidepressants may play an important role in helping a person give up a substance habit.

2 Alcohol treatment

"Getting and staying sober through AA has taught me that life happens and I have to adjust....life just keeps getting better, one day at a time."

"Sylvia", Alcoholics Anonymous

What drugs are available for alcohol abuse?

The three medications available for the treatment of alcohol problems are disulfiram [Antabuse], naltrexone [Nalorex] and Acamprosate [Campral].

Disulfiram

The first drug proven to treat alcohol addiction was disulfiram [Antabuse] which acts, literally, as a deterrent to drinking. Disulfiram does not act on the brain, but it allows the toxic breakdown product of alcohol, acetaldehyde, to accumulate in the body by blocking the enzyme, acetaldehyde dehydrogenase (ADH), which would normally break it down into innocuous acetate. Acetaldehyde is one of the main culprits contributing to a hangover, so someone taking disulfiram can expect unpleasant symptoms such as nausea if they drink. Disulfiram is useful for addicts that are motivated to stay off alcohol, but it can, of course, be tempting not to take the pill at all. On its own, disulfiram is probably of little use to the recovering alcoholic.

Naltrexone

As a mu-opioid antagonist, naltrexone works by taking away the pleasure of drinking – that is, it blocks the receptors in the brain where alcohol acts so that it doesn't have its usual effect. Naltrexone is safe and can be taken as a daily pill. Research in animal models suggests that naltrexone does reduce alcohol drinking.[72a] Clinical trials suggest that naltrexone is better at preventing relapse than placebo.[73] People on naltrexone have fewer episodes of relapse and a higher percentage can remain abstinent after 12 weeks of treatment. However, there is not, as yet, much evidence that it is useful in the long term.

Acamprosate

Taken in oral form, it is not completely clear how this drug works but acamprosate may help restore the balance between inhibitory and excitatory neuronal systems in the nervous system – a balance that is disturbed by chronic alcohol exposure.[73a] Rats bred to drink alcohol reduce their intake on acamprosate. Clinical trials have shown that acamprosate, like naltrexone, is also better than placebo in prolonging abstinence from alcohol.[74] It lengthens time before relapse, (a person stays alcohol-free longer) reduces the number of drinking days and increases complete abstinence among alcohol-dependent patients. A recent analysis suggested that acamprosate might be the preferred "first line" treatment for severe alcohol problems, as it seems to act for longer than naltrexone.[75]

Both naltrexone and acamprosate act on the brain and seem to reduce or even extinguish the psychoactive effects of alcohol and reduce feelings of craving. Unlike disulfiram, they neither enhance the toxic effects of alcohol, if someone lapses, and nor do they have abuse potential in their own right. But how do naltrexone and acamprosate compare? Is one better than the other? Do you get even more benefit from combination therapy? A recent trial carried out by researchers in Hamburg, Germany, provided some answers.[76] Both drugs, used alone, were clearly more effective than placebo in preventing relapse in a 12-week study. And the combination of the two was better than either drug alone – the relapse rate was just 25 per cent, which is lower than similar trials of these drugs used alone.

However, individuals do have to be motivated to get the most from naltrexone or acamprosate; after all, they take away the pleasure of drinking. In this study, medication was supported by a programme of group therapy that the researchers believe was a major contributor to the success of the trial. The therapy focused on anticipating situations that might provoke relapse and developing skills for coping with them.

3 Treatment for smoking

"I've noticed loads of benefits since I stopped smoking. My skin definitely has a bloom and my sense of taste and smell are heaps better."

Fiona Phillips, GMTV presenter, ASH website

How does nicotine replacement work?

For the smoker who is motivated to give up, nicotine replacement therapy (NRT) can help reduce the discomfort of withdrawal symptoms and cravings during the transition to abstinence. NRT, which is available in various forms (see below), provides nicotine – the addictive component of cigarettes – without the accompanying tar, carbon monoxide and other toxins. As such, it is a form of harm reduction. NRT does not produce a "peak" level of nicotine in the blood as rapidly as smoking does and it does not have the accompanying rewarding effects. It is not believed that nicotine in the form of NRT is addictive or open to abuse. NRT is not intended as a full "cure" for smoking, more as an aid to giving up. It is meant as a short-term tool that should be used only for weeks or months, not indefinitely. NRT is available either over-the-counter or on prescription.

- **Nicotine gum.** This was the first form of NRT to be made available and is used in a similar way to cigarettes, i.e. whenever one feels the urge to smoke. There is a stronger, double-dose gum (4 mg) that may be more suitable for heavy smokers. Some people find the taste unpleasant at first.

- **Nicotine patches.** Discreet, nicotine-impregnated patches that stick to the skin. Patches are limiting in that you cannot control the dose to get more nicotine when your craving is stronger. Heavier smokers may be more successful starting off with the higher dose patch. They last either for either 16 hours or 24 hours and should be applied, usually first thing in the morning, to a part of the body where they can't easily be rubbed off.

- **Sublingual microtabs.** These release nicotine into the body through the mucous membranes beneath the tongue and, like gum, come in 2 mg and 4 mg strengths.

- **Sugar-free mint lozenges.** Recently introduced, each lozenge contains 1 mg or 2 mgs of nicotine. Up to 25 (low-dose) lozenges a day can be taken.

- **Inhalator.** A plastic holder, similar to a cigarette holder that has a specially shaped end to hold on to, with nicotine cartridges that fit in the end. You draw on it like a cigarette but the nicotine is absorbed through the mucous membranes of the mouth and throat rather than the lungs.

- **Nasal spray.** This is a nicotine solution that is sprayed up the nose. The nicotine is absorbed more quickly – taking 10 to 15 minutes to reach peak concentrations compared to other formulations which take 30 minutes to reach a peak. It can be used every 30 minutes. Some people, however, find the nasal spray causes irritation.

Does nicotine replacement therapy (NRT) work?

NRT has been widely investigated with clinical trials covering over 28,000 people. These results show that, compared to placebo, smokers on NRT are twice as likely to be abstinent 12 months after deciding to give up.[77]

The results also held true for various sub-groups, such as pregnant women and people with heart disease. Therefore NRT can be considered to be a useful option for smokers across the board. Most of the investigation has been performed on gum and patches, but there's sufficient evidence on the other forms to suggest that all products are equally as effective. It is best to choose the one that fits in best with your individual needs and lifestyle.

While NRT is more effective than placebo in helping people stop smoking, overall quit rates are still woefully low (see page 120) – no more than 20 per cent at best, which is worse than the success rate of giving up any other drug. This may be related to the lack of "reward" associated with NRT – though it does remove the risk of smoking, it takes away the pleasure too. To persist with NRT, the individual has to be truly motivated. Studies have shown that giving support – in the form of face-to-face or telephone counselling might improve the smoker's chance of giving up. For instance, researchers at the University of Vermont, in the US, found that proactive telephone support, delivered by ex-smokers, improved the quit rate of low-income women on nicotine patches from 28 per cent to 42 per cent at three months.[78] However, by six months there was no difference between the two groups, suggesting that perhaps prolonged support is the only way of getting someone to quit in the long-term.

Is nicotine replacement really safe?

Nicotine itself is not without risk – it has an effect on the heart and circulation. It should be used with caution if you have heart disease (especially after a recent heart attack or stroke although, of course, these are essential times to give up smoking), ulcers or gastritis, diabetes and kidney or liver problems. However, it is important to remember that nicotine replacement is still far safer than continuing to smoke in the vast majority of cases.

A few smokers do use nicotine replacements for longer than is recommended, raising the question as to whether these replacement therapies are, in themselves, addictive. This seems unlikely, because the nicotine is not delivered in the same way as in a cigarette and cannot reach a sharp peak concentration in the brain so quickly. It is far less rewarding to the addict than having a smoke. A review of the evidence does suggest that nicotine replacement rarely leads to dependence[79] and such a dependence would, in any case, be less harmful than smoking and easier to break.

Abstinence from smoking after 12 months in patients on nicotine replacement therapy (NRT)

Formulation	Abstinence rates on treatment (%)	Abstinence rates on placebo or no treatment (%)
NRT gum	17.9	11.0
NRT patch	13.5	8.7
NRT inhalator	17.1	9.1
NRT nasal spray	23.8	11.8
NRT sublingual tablet/lozenge	20.1	12.6
Any NRT	17.6	10.3

Information from http://www.nice.org.uk/ (*National Institute for Clinical Excellence Technical Appraisal Guidance 29, 2002*)

Can nicotine replacement therapy be made more successful?

There are many unanswered questions about NRT and smoking cessation. It's not clear what the optimum duration of use is, or whether there's any difference between weaning off smoking or stopping it abruptly. Most studies have not followed people for more than a year after starting NRT and it is important to know whether it works in the long term. Research is also needed to see whether success rates on NRT can really be improved by counselling and, if so, what kinds of counselling work best.

Is there an alternative to nicotine replacement therapy?

Bupropion is a non-nicotine aid to smoking cessation that appears to be at least as successful as NRT. Research suggests that quit rates of 25–49 per cent at six months are achievable on bupropion.[80] A trial comparing bupropion with NRT suggested that bupropion alone or in combination with NRT could be twice as effective as NRT alone or placebo after 12 months.[81]

Bupropion treatment for smoking

Bupropion has been in use as an antidepressant for around 15 years. It is classed as an "atypical" antidepressant, which works by preventing the re-uptake of noradrenaline, dopamine and serotonin, as well as being a nicotine receptor antagonist. Buproprion SR (sustained release) [Zyban] has been developed purely for smoking cessation, after the observation that those treated for depression with the original formulation found it helped them to stop smoking. Bupropion SR works in smokers with and without depression and it's not known whether its anti-smoking action is linked to its antidepressant activity. However, many people who smoke also suffer from depression and it may be that they turn to nicotine to self-medicate. If the depression is treated, then cigarettes may lose their appeal.

Treatment with bupropion starts before the patient stops smoking – typically within two weeks of a target date. It takes about a week for bupropion levels to build up to an effective level. Treatment is for a course of 7–12 weeks. Side-effects are typical of other antidepressants and include dry mouth, headache and insomnia. There is a small risk (one in

1000) that bupropion may induce seizures and it is not recommended for certain patients for that reason. Around the time when bupropion SR was introduced, there was extensive media coverage of some serious adverse effects, including a number of deaths, linked to the drug. The UK Medicines Control Agency says that the contribution of buproprion to the 58 deaths reported since June 2000 remains unproved and underlying conditions – some smoking-related – could have been the cause.[82] Some people continue to believe that buproprion may be very dangerous. Ongoing monitoring since has suggested such events are rare – occurring at about half the average reported rate for new drugs in Britain.[83] Nevertheless, many remain unconvinced of bupropion's safety. As ever, the individual has to weigh up the potential risk with the undeniable health risks of smoking.

Heavy drinking isn't advisable on bupropion because seizures are more likely if you stop drinking quickly. Bupropion should not be prescribed with monoamine oxidase inhibitor antidepressants or for anyone who is already taking it for depression. Anyone taking bupropion together with NRT should do so only under medical supervision, because the combination has been shown to increase blood pressure. As with NRT, it's likely that bupropion has greatest chance of success when used with some form of counselling.

Zyban (bupropion) to the rescue

 I knew smoking was bad for me, but everybody around me was doing it. I thought it was cool and I didn't pay any attention to the health issues at first. It was only when I started smoking more that I began to think about the health risks. And my health really was affected: I was very short of breath, and I hated waking up with that irritating cough that smokers get. I tried to stop two or three times, but I wasn't very successful. I managed to stop for two weeks using nicotine patches, but then I came "unstuck" on holiday.

I knew that to succeed in stopping for good I was going to need help, so I prepared for my next quit attempt by visiting my GP who prescribed a course of Zyban tablets. I started taking these eight days before my stop day. I quit around Christmas time 2000. I'd finished a night shift and had three "ciggies" left, which I smoked on the way home without enjoying any of them. The next morning, the cravings weren't really there. I did feel awkward and unusual, but I could cope with it. Instead of smoking I ate – quite a lot! I put on 14 pounds in two months but I didn't let it bother me. I let myself carry on eating – food was a kind of reward – and I decided to worry about the weight later. Then I started exercising more, as well as dieting and now I've lost it again.

Zyban was really, really good: the tablets took away the craving, although the side-effects were a bit of a problem. I felt very anxious and suffered from headaches and insomnia while taking it, but I persevered. At six weeks I really began to feel healthier. I eat much more healthily these days as well. I have a lot of salads and fish but not as much meat as before. I haven't just given up smoking, I've completely changed my lifestyle. One of my main reasons for stopping smoking was to get healthier and I'm amazed at the improvement since I quit.

When I first stopped smoking, I was worried that I wouldn't be able to cope at work with the stress levels. If we had a busy half-hour, I used to go outside for a cigarette thinking that it relieved the stress. But I actually find that I'm doing my job better now than before. I'm definitely richer since stopping smoking too. Every time I open my wallet, I can't believe how much money is in it! I've already had two holidays on the money I've saved. Just after I finished the Zyban, I went skiing in France, and I've also had a fortnight in Florida.

ASH website, formerly published in *STOP* magazine

Tips for giving up smoking

■ Keep a diary of when you smoke, so you can analyse your smoking habits and prepare to quit. The physical act of recording your habit will remind you of what you are doing.

■ Stop using all forms of tobacco. Don't make the mistake of thinking that light cigarettes or pipes or cigars will be any less harmful. Tobacco is tobacco and it will kill you.

■ Don't worry, be happy and feel good. As an ex-smoker and an ex-drinker you have more chance of feeling good for longer.

■ Make a firm commitment to yourself.

■ Set a quit date and don't stray from it.

■ Think about all your loved ones, especially children if you have them, and know that they depend on you. You owe it to them to stick around for as long as possible.

■ Write down all the benefits of giving up smoking and the drawbacks of continuing to smoke. Put it somewhere where you can see it

■ Remind yourself to keep a positive attitude. Gain something really important by quitting.

■ If you don't want to put on weight, keep plenty of fruit around the house to nibble on.

■ Don't waste your time wondering whether quitting smoking really is the right decision – it is!

■ Remember that it doesn't matter who you are, everyone is capable of giving up smoking.

■ Take some kind of exercise and take up a new hobby. It will reinforce the change you are making in a positive way

■ If you think that smoking is relaxing, then try the Pulse Rate test. Check your pulse before and after having a cigarette and you'll see that smoking really makes your heart race.

■ Taper off the number of cigarettes you smoke.

■ Make it a major lifestyle change and consider giving up (or reducing) the amount of tea and coffee you drink. A bigger change can feel like more of a fresh start, and coffee and tea are closely associated with cigarettes for a great many smokers.

■ If you find that you're eating more and putting on weight, worry about that afterwards – tackle the smoking problem first.

■ Get encouragement from family and friends.

■ Take one day at a time.

■ (for pregnant quitters) Visualize that little life inside you, which is so clean and pure. Remember that if you smoke, you'll be contaminating your baby before he or she even has the chance to breathe fresh air.

■ (for pregnant quitters). Remember that even though quitting can be hard, you do have a choice about whether to smoke or not. Your baby doesn't have that choice.

From ASH website, first published in *STOP* magazine

Are there any other smoking cessation treatments?

Aside from bupropion, there are currently no other drug treatments for smoking cessation that are licensed in the UK or the European Union. However, researchers at Duke University in the US have been studying a drug called mecamylamine, which is a nicotine antagonist originally developed for the treatment of high blood pressure. Two small trials have suggested that mecamylamine enhances the effectiveness of the nicotine patch[84] with success rates up to 40 per cent at one year being reported.

Can acupuncture be used to treat addiction?

It has been suggested that acupuncture stimulates the opioid receptors, leading to the production of endogenous opioids, which is why it can help relieve pain. This theory is backed by various observations, for example, mice lacking opioid receptors do not respond to acupuncture-induced analgesia as normal animals do. A number of clinical trials have shown that acupuncture can ease the process of withdrawal from heroin.[85] Acupuncture is also popular in the treatment of smoking addiction. However, an analysis of 22 trials comparing acupuncture with "sham" acupuncture – in which needles are inserted but not activated (the equivalent of a placebo) – suggests it has little to offer.[86] Complementary and alternative medicine (CAM) may be a helpful adjunct to some of the medical treatments.

Ear acupuncture to treat nicotine addiction. Acupuncture is based on a traditional Chinese treatment. Acupuncture points lie on lines (meridians) along which life energy (Qi) flows. Blocked lines cause disorders, which are treated by the correct positioning of needles or other stimulating devices. Modern science explains the effects by the release of endorphins (the body's painkillers) caused by the stimulation.

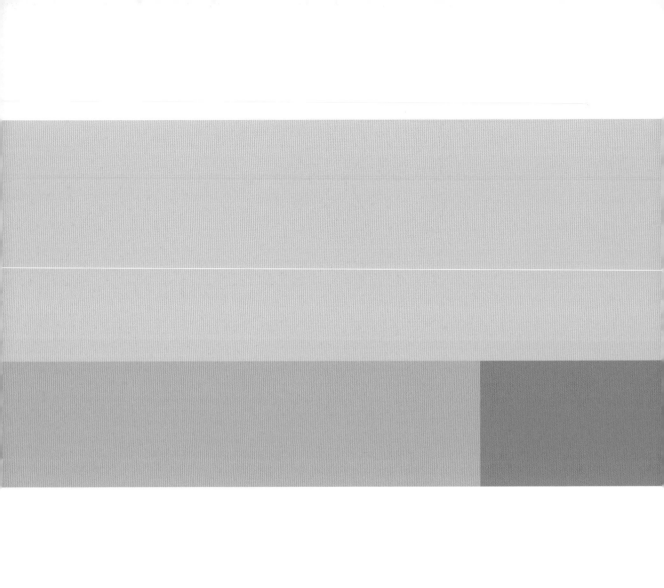

4 Treatment for other addictions

"You learn by your own mistakes. I am only human and to me it is a real achievement to leave drugs alone."

"Sandie", from *Streetwise, Drugwise*, Eva Roman and Richard James, Management Books, 2000

Is there a drug treatment for behavioural addictions?

Drug treatments are sometimes prescribed for behavioural compulsions, such as gambling and shopping. They are probably used less often, however, than they are for substance abuse.

Compulsive gambling has been treated by a range of antidepressant drugs, particularly the selective serotonin reuptake inhibitors such as fluoxetine [Prozac], sertraline [Zoloft] and fluvoaxime [Luvox].[87] These have shown some success against obsessive-compulsive disorder, which is why they may help to reduce the urge to gamble. Another antidepressant, clomipramine [Anafranil] has been reported to reduce the incidence of pathological gambling, while bupropion [Wellbutrin] may be especially helpful for those with a history of depression and attention deficit disorder. Such drugs are particularly useful where the gambler has co-existing mental health problems, or other addictions. But they work best in conjunction with a psychosocial treatment such as the "12-Steps" (see page 141) and individual therapy. Recently, the opioid antagonist naltrexone, which is used to treat alcohol and heroin addiction has also been found to help gamblers in a small placebo-controlled trial.[88] Researchers at the University of Minnesota found that 75 per cent of those on naltrexone reported much reduced gambling urges, compared to only 25 per cent in the placebo group. Similar success has been reported when a group of gamblers were treated with an antidepressant called nefazodone [Serzone].[89] This relatively new drug is not like the SSRIs or any of the other antidepressants in its structure or action and is linked with fewer side-effects, which may make it more acceptable to those struggling to break free of a behavioural addiction.

Is it true that compulsive shopping can be treated with antidepressants?

There have been several reports over the last few years on the use of SSRIs for treating compulsive shopping. In a recent report, researchers at Stanford University, California, found that citalopram [Cipramil] produced good results in a trial involving 24 compulsive shoppers (23 women and one man).[90] First, all received citalopram for seven weeks and 15 reported themselves to be "very much" or "much" improved, in that they'd lost their interest in shopping. The people who responded to the treatment then went on to the second phase of the trial, where they were assigned to either citalopram or placebo. Five out of eight on placebo relapsed, but none of those who continued medication did so. They were no longer interested in the shops, they could go to a shopping centre without buying anything, they no longer browsed the internet or TV shopping channels for things to buy. In other words, they could purchase things normally as and when they needed them.

Incidentally, the authors of this study note that previous trials showed a large placebo response and put this down to asking the shoppers to keep a shopping diary – a process that in itself may be therapeutic (see page 132).

The fact that medication that boosts serotonin levels can help with compulsive behaviours such as gambling suggests that treating an underlying depressive disorder is, in itself, therapeutic. Where serotonin levels are low, there is often a tendency towards impulsive behaviour, which may be an important component of the depression and the driver behind the compulsive behaviour. Normalizing serotonin levels, along with therapy that provides insights and an opportunity to learn new behaviour patterns, may be enough set the individual on the road to recovery.

Shopping diary

Use these pages to make notes of the circumstances under which you most feel compelled to shop. Often simply jotting down habits can help you identify addictive behaviour patterns.

Emotion	Monday	Tuesday	Wednesday
sad/ depressed			
happy/ things are looking up			
frustrated/ bored			
unhappy in your job			
lacking self-esteem			

	Thursday	Friday	Saturday	Sunday

Don't most people relapse once their treatment has ended?

Stopping an addictive drug or behaviour in the short-term is actually relatively easy. Staying clear (or "clean" as many addicts put it) is far more difficult. Relapse is only another drink, hit or bet away, however long someone has stayed free of addiction (which may be why complete abstinence is often advocated as the only approach to addiction).

One study of people who had withdrawn from opiates under an in-treatment programme revealed that within only one week, half had returned to opiate use on at least one occasion.[91] Within six weeks, nearly three-quarters admitted using opiates. Does this mean the treatment was a complete waste of time for the majority? No, because longer follow-up showed that during the six months after leaving treatment, there was a gradual increase in the numbers who were opiate-free, including many of those who had initially returned to drug use. At the six- month point, about half the group were abstinent from opiates and other drugs. Had the study focused upon initial relapse, then it would certainly have been judged a failure. It is important to distinguish between a lapse or slip, and relapse. For many, lapses are part of the fluctuating chronic nature of addiction. They must be admitted, faced up to, dealt with, and then moved on from. People who avoid relapse are those with protective factors in their environment such as a support network (family and/or an ongoing self-help group like Alcoholics Anonymous), activities (group meetings, new hobbies, a job) or social structure. Psychological treatment, especially cognitive behaviour therapy, (see page 152–157) can also do a great deal to protect against relapse.

In a recent study, a group of 242 clients receiving residential treatment for heroin addiction were followed for 12 months.[92] Soon after treatment ended, 60 per cent had lapsed. The researchers divided the group into three: relapsers (still using heroin at 12 months), lapsers (had lapsed, then become abstinent) and abstainers (had not lapsed). The abstinent and lapsed groups, who avoided the full relapse, reported more use of cognitive, avoidance and distraction strategies; lapsed and relapse groups, however, reported higher use of illicit drugs other than heroin (such as cannabis) than abstainers (in this context, people who were abstinent from heroin – they may still, however, have been taking other drugs).

How can relapse be prevented by therapy?

Relapse prevention (RP) therapy should, ideally, be tailored to the individual patient and his or her history of drug-taking, or addictive behaviour. This involves identifying the "high risk" situations that the patient will face after treatment – be it a specific group of friends who will offer drugs, the pub, the racetrack or the shopping mall. The therapist and patient will look together at past successes and failures and what factors might have contributed to these. Research has suggested that a patient who is willing to take personal responsibility for failures and who believes that he or she has control over relapse is more likely to achieve the desired state of abstinence.[93]

A detailed analysis of high-risk situations is central to therapy. It is important to look at the situations that might arise and to develop skills for dealing with them (don't go to the pub, go but don't drink, don't sit with a certain group and so on). Fostering an attitude of self-belief in the patient, which is core to cognitive behaviour therapy (CBT), is particularly relevant to RP, as is dealing with negative mood states such as anxiety and depression that may trigger relapse.

Some approaches to RP have involved deliberately exposing the patient to cues to drug-taking behaviour and helping them deal with the feelings these evoke. This allows the patient to face up to cravings in the hope that they will eventually be extinguished. Another line to take is the "Samurai" approach in which the craving is treated as an enemy that can be vanquished by preparing for the attack. Another important element of RP is to help the patient realize that all is not lost if they lapse, but to quickly regain control of their lives. An analysis of all the evidence – covering nearly 10,000 participants – shows that the best application of the RP approach could be for alcohol and polysubstance abuse, especially in conjunction with anti-craving medications.[94]

Story of a lapse

 The rehabilitation programme lasts for 12 months in total but Lindsay decided after seven months that he had lost his commitment to the programme, but not to himself. He wanted to get on with his life outside. He had learned to take responsibility, so he discharged himself with the blessing of the centre.

Unable to reach his sister's home on the evening of his discharge, he made his way down to some arches by the river where he and his group used to hang out. It was July and a warm night. Lindsay recalls: "I had flashbacks of my previous life; and then, amazingly, I found some heroin in my pocket that had been there for eight months. I took it and promptly crashed out. When I woke up I felt totally and completely disgusted with myself for letting myself down. After that, I never touched the stuff again. It was the waking up in those surroundings which made me feel that I hadn't progressed at all, and that was the real turning point. "

Streetwise, Drugwise, **Eva Roman and Richard James, Management Books, 1998**

What is the relapse prevention model?

At one time, relapse into a drug or behavioural habit was counted as failure by both the patient and those trying to help them. Then, in the mid-1980s, Alan Marlatt and Judith Gordon presented their theory of relapse prevention (RP), which puts the issue of relapse at the centre of our understanding of addiction and its treatment.[95] Addiction is seen as a collection of bad habits – of both thought and behaviour – and the focus of RP is to maintain positive changes in thoughts and behaviour that occur through treatment. This means preventing the occurrence of initial lapses and, if they occur (as they almost certainly will), preventing them from escalating into total relapse.

The focus of RP is on:

■ Identifying high-risk situations.
■ Developing coping strategies for high-risk situations.

High-risk situations are situations, events, objects, thoughts, mood states that are linked to drug use or relapse. They can include depression, anxiety, boredom, social pressure, social network, inter-personal conflict, ill health. Exposure to drug-related stimuli – a favourite pub, the smoking room at work, or a location where you might have shared drugs with someone – are often very high risk (which may be why the "geographical" cure cited by many who have given up drugs can be so powerful). Even good moods can bring about a relapse – wanting to celebrate an event or achievement with a drink or a cigarette can be hard to resist.

Coping strategies include social-skills training and more global coping skills such as lifestyle balance. The client learns to deal with craving as a wave that they can ride and not something they are powerless to resist.

Attitude towards lapses are important in RP – it's important to take responsibility but when this becomes overloaded with guilt and a sense of failure, the lapse is more likely to become a full-blown relapse. The therapist can help the client see that they are not powerless over their own behaviour. It is always possible to learn from mistakes.

RP models and treatments have been applied to a wide range of addictive behaviours including drug addiction, alcoholism, HIV risk behaviours, eating disorders, compulsive sexual disorders, anger control, gambling – in fact most problems involving a lack of impulse control.

What happens at Alcoholics Anonymous?

Alcoholics Anonymous (AA) is a self-help movement that was founded in the USA in 1935 by Bob Smith and Bob Wilson as a result of their own experiences with alcohol abuse. They developed the now famous "12 Step" programme (see page 141) that forms the basis of the movement's philosophy. AA now operates in 134 countries around the world and it is estimated that there are around 40,000 – 50,000 AA members in the UK alone.

In brief, the AA view of addiction is based around the following:

- Addiction involves a loss of control over one's behaviour, despite an awareness of the harm it does to oneself and others.
- Addiction is a lifelong condition (once an alcoholic, always an alcoholic – even if you have not touched a drink for years).
- Abstinence is the only cure for addiction.
- Addiction is an illness (though not necessarily a brain disorder, as outlined in this book; no one specific cause is promoted).
- The individual remains fully responsible for the consequences of their addictive behaviour and for their own recovery.

Recovery occurs through the support of the group. Members are encouraged to go to meetings, which are free, where they share their history, experiences and feelings with others. While a member is sharing, others are asked not to interrupt and are not allowed to offer either advice or criticism. This is to promote a non-judgemental, accepting attitude which can help someone to change. The "12-step" approach involves more than giving up drink – it asks for a fundamental shift in the way one views oneself and others (similar, in many ways, to the aims of cognitive behaviour therapy – see page 152–157). Between meetings, support from other members is available by phone, post or email. A valuable component of the AA approach is sponsoring, where one alcoholic who is further down the road to recovery will act as a mentor to a new member. Sponsoring or mentoring can be a valuable and therapeutic learning experience for both parties.

The "12-step" approach has been applied to substance abuse and Narcotics Anonymous and Cocaine Anonymous groups are now widespread. Gamblers Anonymous exists to support compulsive gamblers. Support for family members is also available through Al-Anon and related groups.

A "TEMPORARY SPONSOR" (OF THE SAME GENDER) IS A VERY IMPORTANT THING.

The 12 Steps of Alcoholics Anonymous

1. We admitted we were powerless over alcohol – that our lives had become unmanageable.
2. We came to believe that a power greater than ourselves could restore us to sanity.
3. We made a decision to turn our will and our lives over to the care of God as we understood him.
4. We made a searching and fearless moral inventory of ourselves.
5. We admitted to God, to ourselves, and to another human being the exact nature of our wrongs.
6. We were entirely ready to have God remove all the defects of character.
7. We humbly asked Him to remove our shortcomings.
8. We made a list of all persons we had harmed and became willing to make amends to them all.
9. We made direct amends to such people wherever possible, except when to do so would injure them or others.
10. We continued to take personal inventory and when we were wrong promptly admitted it.
11. We sought through prayer and meditation to improve our conscious contact with God as we understood Him, praying only for knowledge of His will for us and the power to carry that out.
12. Having had a spiritual awakening as a result of these steps, we tried to carry this message to alcoholics, and to practise these principles in all our affairs.

Despite the apparent religious element of the 12 Steps there are elements that can be adapted to any person's belief system. The mention of "God" can be taken to emphasize our vulnerability, and the fact that we are all, more or less, a product of our environment and subject to the world around us – good and bad.

Does the 12-step approach to addiction actually work?

It is not easy to evaluate the "12-step" approach in the same way as treatment with a psychological or drug treatment given in a clinical setting. The closed and self-selected nature of the group and the guaranteed anonymity make it hard for health professionals to penetrate the AA culture (although some meetings are open to non-members). As a result, little formal research has been done on AA and even less on related organizations. A recent review of the evidence, however, suggests that AA is effective in maintaining abstinence in the long term and recommends that physicians become more familiar with AA methods. [96]

The advantages of AA are easy to see. It's free, open to all who want to tackle their addiction, flexible and widely available. Support from AA is long term and often at times when other help is not available. It is compatible with other forms of treatment. However, treatments such as methadone maintenance for opiate addiction are fundamentally at odds with the "12-step" philosophy because they focus on harm reduction, not abstinence. The "12-step" approach is not, however, for everyone. Some object to its apparently "religious" focus, even though people are free to interpret "God" in whatever way has personal meaning (the power of love, the "higher" self, nature, the group, etc.). Others may dislike the idea of sharing intimate experiences and feelings with strangers and prefer to work one-to-one with a professional or attempt to give up their addiction through their own efforts.

See NEWSWEEK COVER STORY March 3, 2008 EDITION — VACCINE FOR ADDICTIONS?

Will there be a vaccine against addiction?

Research over the last decade or so has shown that it might be possible to produce effective vaccines against diseases such as cancer and drug addiction. All vaccines rely on activating one or more parts of the immune system so that it is better able to fight the disease.

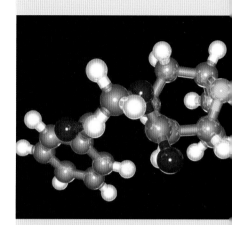

The next few years might see the introduction of vaccines against cocaine and nicotine. These are already in human clinical trials and development is underway on vaccines against phencyclidine, methamphetamine and heroin.

This artwork of a cocaine molecule shows the structure of this molecule, which allows certain compounds to bind to it. This idea forms the basis of scientific investigations into possible vaccinations.

Antibodies are a key component of the immune system and many vaccines – including addiction vaccines – work by stimulating antibody production in the body. In the case of an addiction vaccine, the antibodies will lock on to the drug molecule as soon as it enters the body. Antibodies are large protein molecules that cannot cross the blood-brain barrier, so the drug, once bound to its antibody, cannot enter into the brain and so cannot activate the brain's reward system. In animal studies, cocaine and nicotine vaccines reduced the self-administration of these drugs. One clinical trial of the cocaine vaccine has shown that 58 per cent of users were able to give up during a three-month follow-up, while another study had three-quarters of recent quitters staying off cocaine after being vaccinated.[97]

Cocaine is a small molecule that is not usually "seen" by the immune system. In the cocaine vaccine, the drug is linked to a much bigger molecule, which the immune system will recognize: the non-toxic part of the cholera toxin. This enables the immune system to respond, as if the cocaine were an invading virus, such as measles or smallpox, and manufacture anti-cocaine antibodies. These are large protein molecules that lock onto the cocaine, forming a complex that's too big to cross over the blood-brain barrier; if cocaine can't reach the brain, then the user can't get any pleasure from it.

There are a number of challenges with the vaccine approach to drug treatment. It is not clear whether a vaccine will have an effect on cravings or on withdrawal symptoms – both of which can reinstate drug-seeking behaviour. Many people may be interested in the idea of vaccinating young people, so that they never start taking heroin or cocaine. But would this be ethical? Another problem is that people vary in their ability to produce antibodies – some may produce too few, so that part of a dose of drug does reach the brain. And since vaccines are specific, there would be nothing to stop someone turning to another drug for a hit.

As with other treatments, the vaccines will probably work best in highly motivated individuals who are in a comprehensive programme with both medication and psychosocial support elements tailored to their needs. For most people with a drug problem, this will mean attending a specialist clinic or agency where a team of social workers, psychologists and clinicians will, ideally, work together to provide therapy.

A new approach to treating cocaine addiction

Researchers at the Scripps Research Institute in California designed an antibody that could bind to cocaine molecules several years ago. This "mops up" cocaine in the system and stops it getting to the brain (because the antibody molecule is too big to pass through the blood-brain barrier). Animal studies showed this approach to be limited, as a large dose of cocaine overwhelmed the antibody dose and the excess leaked into the brain. Now, however, the team has found a way round this.[98] They have modified the cocaine antibody so it can enter the brain and soak up cocaine that has crossed the blood-brain barrier. They have inserted the gene for the antibody into a virus called a filamentous phage, which normally infects bacteria. When the phage particles are grown, they have hundreds of antibody molecules on their surfaces. The particles can enter the brain through a nasal spray and the antibodies then lock onto any cocaine molecules, blocking their effect. So far, the treatment has been shown to inhibit one effect of cocaine in animal models – increased movement of the animals as a result of the stimulating effect of the drug. This suggests that the method could work – although it will be some time before it is ready for testing in humans. It is encouraging to see that the most advanced techniques in molecular biology are now being applied to the treatment of drug addiction.

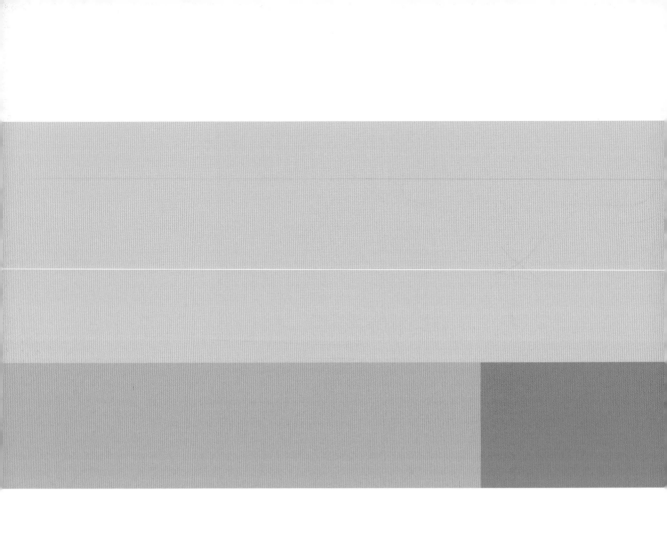

5 CBT and other treatments

"Relapses will occur; there is no perfect preventative.
The most important thing is for relapse to be contained."

Dr Avram Goldstein, *Addiction: From Biology to Drug Policy,*
Oxford University Press, *2001*

Can psychological therapies help beat addiction?

Today there's a range of psychological treatments that can help to treat drug addiction. Increasingly, there's a move away from confrontation – where the therapist tells the client to stop using drugs – and towards a partnership where they work together to look at the problem.

Modern psychological treatments look more at what can be done in the present, rather than analysing what went wrong in the past to contribute to an addiction problem. There's a big emphasis on changing behaviour – as described in discussions of cognitive behavioural therapy. Developing practical skills, such as finding ways of coping with potential relapse, is also important. The client-centred approach has led to a new interest in motivation for change and how to support it. And there is an increasing trend towards looking at what can be done to help a client in just a few minutes, or one session. Added to this, psychological therapies can be combined with medication to enhance the chances of success. There is also still a lot that the addict can do for him- or herself – so much so that many harness their natural internal healing capacity to recover without any therapy at all.

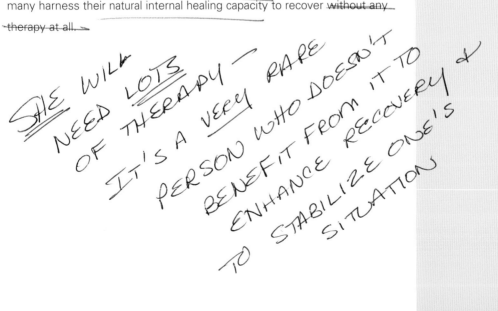

SHE WILL NEED LOTS OF THERAPY – IT'S A VERY RARE PERSON WHO DOESN'T BENEFIT FROM IT TO ENHANCE RECOVERY & TO STABILIZE ONE'S SITUATION

What kinds of therapy are available for the treatment of addiction?

A wide range of psychological treatments can be used to help tackle substance or behavioural abuse. These range from straightforward counselling and cognitive behavioural therapy (CBT) through to brief therapy and motivational treatments.

Psychological treatment for addiction might be delivered in a variety of settings – as group therapy or individual therapy, for instance, on an out-patient or in-patient basis, in the private sector or in the health service. Therapy may be given alongside some kind of pharmacological treatment (such as bupropion for smoking cessation, or methadone for opiate addiction) and other types of help may be offered if appropriate (for example with housing, employment, or relationships). The therapist may be a psychiatrist, a nurse with special training, a psychotherapist or a social worker (never be afraid to ask your therapist about his or her qualifications). Apart from appropriate qualifications, perhaps the most important factor in a therapist is some degree of genuine empathy for the patient. Improvement is unlikely if the patient feels that the therapist disapproves of them or is patronizing.

The overall goal of therapy may be either total abstinence or harm reduction. There is also a difference between the techniques and support needed during initial change (giving up the addiction and withdrawal problem) and maintenance (avoiding relapse). Addiction is a long-term or even lifelong problem for many people but it is not usually practical to have years of therapy – although it may be possible to find ongoing support. The therapy needs to help the patient acquire skills that will put them back in control of their lives and keep them free of addiction. The most popular approach to addiction therapy in recent years is probably CBT.

What is harm reduction?

only when there is NO other choice

Abstinence may be the ideal goal for someone with a serious drug problem, but it may not be seen as achievable (or even desirable). As we have seen, relapse is common in drug abuse and abstinence may take years to achieve. Meanwhile, drugs – or, more usually, associated factors – continue to pose a risk both to the user and to society as a whole. That is why the more pragmatic approach of harm reduction (or harm minimization) has been set alongside the ideal of abstinence in recent years.

Harm reduction came to the forefront in the mid-1980s with the advent of HIV infection, which can be spread by sharing drug injecting equipment. Since then, it has become clear that hepatitis C can also be spread by sharing needles for the injection of drugs. In fact, even prior to the discovery of HIV, harm reduction approaches had been advocated by some practitioners – suggesting, for instance, that opiate addicts be given injectable heroin under medical supervision (rather than oral methadone) to save them from the risks of injecting illict drugs. Harm reduction involves measures such as:

- Needle exchange schemes to ensure those at risk have access to sterile equipment.
- Advice on safer injecting techniques.
- Provision of facilities for safe disposal of used injecting equipment.
- Advice on safe sex and provision of free condoms to prevent the spread of HIV.

Harm reduction is just a process or approach rather than a treatment. In 1988, The Advisory Council on Misuse of Drugs took the bold step of declaring that, since HIV infection was more harmful to individuals and public health than drug abuse, it was time to adopt a series of harm reduction measures. These were to begin with provision of sterile injecting equipment with the understanding that injecting equipment was not to be shared. The next stage would be to persuade addicts to stop injecting and then, finally, move towards abstinence.[99] In other words, harm reduction is not an alternative to abstinence but a stage on the way towards it.

Needle exchange remains controversial – for widespread provision of sterile equipment may encourage greater rates of injecting which, in turn, will produce more severe drug dependence. In addition there will always be people who choose to share equipment.

It is debatable if needle exchange has reduced HIV infection in the UK, given the time between first infection and diagnosis (which is about ten years for young adults). But there is strong evidence that harm reduction may have been effective as rates of HIV infection among drug users in the UK are lower than in countries that have not adopted such policies.[100, 101]

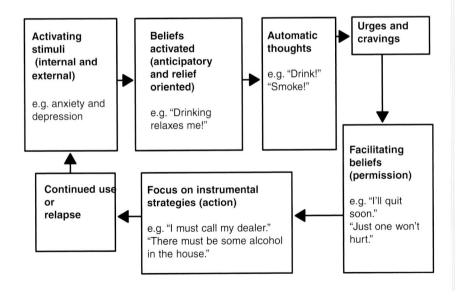

The cognitive model of substance abuse, adapted from Beck's model of cognitive therapy. Beck's cognitive models are applicable to many conditions, including anxiety disorders and depression as well as addiction. Cognitive therapy aims to break negative cycles, placing emphasis on collaboration between therapist and patient/ client.

Are there other forms of harm reduction?

Harm reduction is a wide-reaching and varied approach that is continually being improved. Drugs such as Ecstasy can cause severe dehydration and a high temperature; some clubs provide free water and "chill out" rooms to prevent people getting overheated. Methadone treatment and nicotine replacement therapy can also be seen as harm-reduction measures – protecting addicts from the most harmful aspects of illicit heroin and cigarettes respectively.

Perhaps the best form of harm reduction is to provide people with information on the risks they are running – such as warnings on cigarette packets, or leaflets available in pubs on safe drinking.

Legal and social measures can play an important role in harm reduction. Deaths through drunk driving have fallen dramatically since drink-driving legislation was brought in. Pubs can be designed so that alcohol-fuelled violence is less likely – plastic glasses, a food menu, a more "female-friendly" atmosphere may all help prevent the culture of binge-drinking and irresponsible drinking behaviour.

What is cognitive behaviour therapy (CBT)?

CBT is a form of psychotherapy which combines cognitive therapy and behaviour therapy. It gives a much simpler explanation of emotional problems than psychoanalysis – it is about what we think and what we do and how these things impact on what we feel.

In early psychoanalysis, Sigmund Freud (1856–1939) attempted to explain the patient's/client's condition by analysing his or her past and unconscious. Critics say classical psychoanalysis focuses too much on the problem (and the past) and not enough on the solution (and the future).

Behaviour therapists maintain that by changing behaviour, they can change thoughts; cognitive therapists maintain that by changing thoughts they can change behaviour. They're both right. In fact, both kinds of therapy are practised in combination, to a greater or lesser degree. The terms "cognitive therapy" (CT) and "cognitive behaviour therapy" (CBT) are, in essence, interchangeable.

What happens in CBT?

Undergoing CBT is not like being a patient in the traditional sense, instead, you work in partnership with your therapist. One way of seeing it is that you, the patient, are a kind of researcher working in close collaboration with another researcher (your therapist) to identify and resolve a problem. Your thoughts and beliefs about your addiction make up a scientific hypothesis or idea that is tested by the collection and evaluation of data – just as in a scientific study. This approach suits many people, as it is in line with one of the defining trends in modern healthcare. With the spread of healthcare information via the internet, the emergence of powerful patient advocacy groups, and a general awareness of healthy living, the patient has ceased to be just a passive recipient. Together, therapist and patient identify unhelpful thoughts, beliefs and thought patterns and work out some alternative interpretations. The patient will be encouraged to do "homework" and keep a diary of events, thoughts and ideas. Before the programme starts, therapist and patient agree goals and ground rules – there are many techniques that can be used, and a good therapist will not work by the "rule book" but will adapt the sessions to the patient's strengths and weaknesses.

Psychotherapy sets out to change or modify:

■ Feelings

■ Perceptions

■ Attitudes

■ Behaviour

■ Cognitions
  (thoughts)

But CBT doesn't help everyone, does it? What are the potential problems?

Some people are more likely to fare better than others. It's crucial, for instance, that the patient accepts responsibility (not blame) for his or her situation and will at least accept the possibility of change. The "psychologically minded" client, who has at least minimal insight into their thoughts and feelings, is likely to respond.

Other potentially difficult areas include:

■ ***Homework***: This is a prerequisite of some forms of CBT and some patients are not used to writing and feel shy or embarrassed from lack of practice or fear of spelling mistakes. They may also think their thoughts are too silly to write down.

■ ***Lack of awareness of thoughts or feelings***: Some people find it hard to capture their thoughts or may intellectualize their feelings. These barriers can be overcome – but the patient must be willing to try.

■ **The *"know it all"***: A patient may be so afraid of therapy and concerned about their privacy that they defend themselves by acting as if they know better than the therapist. They may declare themselves "cured" after only one session whereas, in reality, they have hardly scratched the surface of their problem.

■ ***The dependent patient:*** At the other extreme is the patient who is reluctant to stop treatment, fearing they can't maintain freedom from addiction on their own. This can often be overcome by offering appointments at increasing intervals (and pointing out ongoing sources of support).

How is CBT applied to drug misuse?

The philosophy of CBT as applied to addiction is centred around the following ideas:[102]

- Drug misuse arises from both behavioural and cognitive processes that have gone awry.
- Drug misuse is a learned behaviour.
- Drug misuse and the underlying behavioural and cognitive processes are highly modifiable.
- A major goal of CBT is the acquisition of coping skills that will help the patient resist drug taking and reduce any problems associated with it.
- CBT needs a comprehensive and individualized approach so that appropriate techniques are selected.

Techniques used in CBT in the context of addiction are always based on the present and focus on coping with the patient's specific problems (such as how to respond when offered heroin). As with all CBT, it's assumed that it is faulty thought-patterning (cognitions) that drives drug-seeking behaviour. Both behaviour and cognition are the focus of treatment because it's believed that they go hand in hand – that is, cognitive change ("I don't need a drink to relax") will lead to behavioural change ("I'll go to the cinema, rather than the pub, to switch off"). And a change in behaviour (choosing not to buy heroin) drives a change in cognition ("I can get through the day without a hit").

What kind of techniques are used in CBT for addiction?

The therapist should be selective, choosing those techniques that are going to be most relevant to that client and their specific problem. For instance, if someone is troubled by cravings, then distraction and relaxation can help them to stop acting on the urge. Other people may need help in dealing with negative moods that come along with abstention. Techniques that are often used in CBT include:

■ Helping the patient to identify and challenge negative or distorted thought patterns.

■ Keeping a diary that challenges thoughts about their addiction and accompanying behaviour.

■ Behavioural challenges, for example going to a party and not drinking. These should be kept simple and achievable so the patient gets a sense of mastery that will carry them through to the next challenge.

■ Planning ahead for dealing with risky situations, for example, how to avoid places, people and activities associated with drug taking, how to deal with negative feelings, or boredom, finding substitute activities.

■ Distraction and thought stopping – learn to say "no" to intrusive thoughts.

■ Guided imagery – seeing negative rather than positive consequences from drug taking or destructive behaviours (a row with your partner after gambling rather than a big win).

■ Relaxation techniques – learning how to feel good in ways which don't involve your addictive substance.

How successful is CBT for addiction?

In one study, Project MATCH (Matching Alcoholism Treatment to Client Heterogeneity), CBT was compared to 12-Step Facilitation and Motivational Enhancement (see page 141) in a group of 1,500 American problem drinkers.[103] By the end of the trial, 41 per cent of both those in the CBT group and those in the 12-step group were either abstinent or drank moderately. The success rate for those in the motivational enhancement group was only 28 per cent. However, there was little difference between the groups at one-and three-year follow-up. It wasn't possible to pick out those clients who were likely to do best with CBT in the long term.

Another study showed that the success of CBT can be enhanced by naltrexone.[104] A group of 131 recently abstinent alcoholics received 12 weekly sessions of CBT along with either naltrexone or placebo. Those on naltrexone drank less, took longer to relapse and had a longer time between lapses. They also reported more resistance to alcohol-linked thoughts and urges. Over the period of this study, 62 per cent in the naltrexone group did not relapse into heavy drinking, compared with 40 per cent in the placebo group. The study suggests a useful synergy between CBT and naltrexone.

What other psychological treatments are there for addiction?

Traditionally, it has been assumed that an addict is either motivated to change or not. Examples of the latter include those who present for treatment because they are under pressure from their loved ones or through a court order. However, a model of behavioural change that has been developed by Jim Prochaska and Carlo DiClemente in 1985 is centred around the concept that motivation is a fluid property and assumptions should not be made. Most of those wanting treatment will be ambivalent about the process. Those who have come of their own accord will still have mixed feelings about giving up something that, at least at the start, gave life pleasure and meaning. And those who have been coerced may still have some positive feelings at the prospect of a life free of addiction, even if they don't want to do the work of giving up.

Motivational interviewing (MI) is a form of therapy that was developed by William Miller in the USA in 1982 following the Prochaska/ DiClementi model, which has the following stages.[105] At any one time, an addict can be at any stage:

- **Precontemplation:** the user knows the danger of their habit but somehow doesn't relate it to themselves.
- **Contemplation:** first thoughts about giving up or cutting down. Some people move back and forth between precontemplation and contemplation many times before moving on.
- **Preparation:** critical analysis of the habit, perhaps focusing on the pros and cons (cost, health, beating stress).
- **Action:** the person does something, joins AA or buys nicotine patches.
- **Maintenance:** the person engages in activities to maintain the situation – more AA meetings or frequenting non-smoking environments.

In MI, the therapist will take into account the stage the person is at, helping them move forwards. It focuses upon ambivalence and has the following components:

- Labelling is discouraged.
- The patient takes responsibility for his or her recovery while the therapist guides his or her decisions.
- Ambivalence is explored with the therapist encouraging an awareness of dissonance between the patient's behaviour and their ideals; this has to be done in a subtle or skilled way so the patient does not feel coerced and develop resistance, which will prolong the therapy or make it ineffective.

Increasing the patient's self-esteem is key to MI; he or she must realize the great potential for positive change they carry within themselves. MI is especially relevant at the early stages of addiction treatment when ambivalence is at its height and it is important to explore just how ready the patient is to change. It differs from other forms of psychological treatment in that the therapist does not try to persuade or convince the patient to change. Unless carried out by a skilled therapist, this method can seem unfocused.

What's the success rate of motivational interviewing?

MI has been applied to a wide range of substance abuse and other health problems. One review of MI applied to substance abuse (drugs and alcohol), smoking, HIV risk behaviours, and diet/exercise showed at least one improvement in behavioural outcomes – less drug seeking, better diet, more exercise, less risky behaviour in the context of HIV (safer sex) in at least 60 per cent of 29 trials.[106] When used with substance abusers, nearly three-quarters of the trials showed significantly positive outcomes. However, it's still not clear which type of patient benefits from MI. The techniques of MI are often used within the context of brief therapy, so it would be interesting to see just how short a course of MI is needed to trigger long-lasting change.

Does psychological therapy always involve many sessions?

Sometimes, just a few moments of advice and information can set someone on the road to giving up a bad habit. Increasingly, health professionals are being urged to use any contact opportunity to talk to patients about their use of harmful substances. Minimal intervention, as it's known, may involve as little as five minutes or as much as 30 minutes contact time.

The advantage of minimal intervention is that it reaches people who might not otherwise get any opportunity for help. An added advantage is that health-care professionals do not need a great deal of extra training (although they will need some) to deliver minimal intervention. Even if overall success rates are low, the number of interactions between health professionals (doctors, nurses, social workers, pharmacists and so on) and those with an addiction problem is potentially so great that many people stand to benefit.[107] For instance, if someone injures themselves as a result of an alcoholic episode and ends up in an accident and emergency ward, a nurse or doctor could spend five minutes or so – perhaps while "patching him or her up" – giving advice about the risks of alcohol, asking them about their drinking habits and giving information on where to get help, perhaps in written form for them to look at later.

However, if minimal intervention is to be effective, it needs to be undertaken in a non-judgemental, empathic way. Five minutes is not long to assess what kind of help or information a person needs and what is offered may turn out to be inappropriate. Minimal intervention has the capacity to damage the doctor/nurse–patient relationship too if handled insensitively.

Are there any other types of "quick" therapy?

Minimal intervention is a simple and very informal way of helping people with alcohol and other drug problems – it involves measures such as advice, information and perhaps asking someone to monitor their habits. In one study of this approach, one group of men and women who drank to excess was given information about alcohol and asked to keep a drink diary, while a similar group received the usual care – that is, medical attention when they needed it. In the first group, there was a 44 per cent fall in excessive drinking, compared to a 26 per cent decrease in the control group.[108] However, little is known about the type of person most likely to respond to a few words of friendly advice. There's also little evidence on the impact of minimal intervention in the long-term; it may be that people just forget the advice they've been given unless there is some kind of follow-up.

Brief therapy is another approach that can bridge the gap between a minimal intervention and more formal therapies of the type described above. It involves three or four one hour counselling sessions and typically focuses on specific aspects such as motivation, goal setting and self-monitoring to teach the patient skills that will help them change.

Giving up – motivation

Some people will have achieved long periods of abstinence from their addictive substance without outside help. Often something unusual or untoward can trigger a serious relapse and it is important to be aware of an addict's susceptibility to relapsing. Motivation is often key to helping sufferers give up their damaging behaviour.

In one study of 101 heroin addicts who had chosen to give up, one-quarter to one-third did so because they had reached "rock bottom" and desperately needed to find a way out of a crisis.[109] Around two thirds made a rational and explicit decision to stop, while a minority of around five per cent just "drifted away" from drug taking. These individuals chose not to have treatment because they thought they could manage alone, they didn't think treatment would work or they didn't want to be stigmatized by it. Many said that moving away, geographically, from the location where drug taking had originated was the key factor in success. Of course, not everyone has the resources to just get up and leave the area of harm, but this research showed that some individuals could leave "harm's way" in a symbolic way and transform themselves into "non-users" in the same environment, a change that involves the difficult challenge of cutting out former friends and associates. Some dealt with cravings by occasional use of opiates, others used marijuana and alcohol. Many became very health conscious. The study also showed (see page 26–27) that former addicts are very different in their characters and lifestyles and many live basically "straight" lives.

What can someone do to help themselves when undergoing treatment for an addiction?

Treatments such as cognitive behaviour therapy place a clear focus on self-help: learning and practising new skills to help people live free from addiction. The more informal self-help practices that people use to drive their recovery are, perhaps, less well-recognized. One study reveals that in a group of 642 patients in treatment for drug or alcohol addiction, 78 per cent were also using one or more methods of self-help.[110] The most popular methods were:

■ Cutting down (e.g. alternating soft drinks with alcoholic ones).

■ Changing the type or form of substance (beer instead of whisky).

■ Moving house or job.

■ Seeing different friends/making new ones.

■ Joining a self-help group.

Can addiction ever be a positive thing?

The concept of "positive addiction" was described by William Glasser, who argued that activities such as running and meditation lead to a relaxed and energized state of mind[111] without causing any harm to the brain or body. Exercise may not give as powerful a high as heroin, but it still releases endorphins and has many other tangible benefits (and, yes, as already mentioned, exercise "addiction" has been reported but such cases seem to be rare).

It is vital to have some pleasurable and fulfilling activities to take over the void left by giving up an addictive pursuit. AA members have meetings to substitute for pub time (there is no limit on the number of meetings you can go to and they're all free). You can also divert some of the money saved from freeing yourself from addiction into stress-relieving treatments such as massage or meditation. Other people take up creative pleasures such as gardening, reading, or look for new social activities and relationships.

Avoiding risk

As anyone who's tried to give up smoking knows, certain situations like visiting the pub are high risk, because having a drink is a powerful cue to having a cigarette. For those coping with an addiction either on their own or with treatment, the following "stimulus control" techniques might be helpful:

- Get rid of all items linked to your addiction – ashtrays, corkscrews, credit cards, etc.
- Vary your routine – meet friends for coffee on a Saturday morning instead of for a drink on Friday night.
- Go for a swim or a long walk instead of going to the pub or shopping.
- Do you have a favourite chair where you smoke a joint/cigarette/ have a drink? Try rearranging your living room so the associations are lost.

Complementary and alternative therapies for addiction[112]

Therapy	Comments
Acupuncture	Limited evidence for effectiveness in opiate and cocaine dependence anecdotal evidence for smoking
Biofeedback (relaxation method where decreased tension linked to an audible signal through a sensor placed on the skin)	Some evidence for effectiveness in alcohol and cocaine dependence
Electrostimulation (a very small electrical current is passed through the skull)	No evidence for effectiveness in cocaine or opiate addiction
Kudzu	Kudzu (pueraris lobata) a chinese herbal remedy reduces alcohol intake in animal experiments, but not found effective in humans
Hypnotherapy (induction of trance to produce deep relaxation)	One trial showed some impact on alcohol dependence, but failed to distinguish those who were and were not susceptible to hypnosis
Relaxation, yoga, aromatherapy, reflexology	No convincing evidence for effectiveness for opiate addiction
Exercise	Adding exercise to standard therapy for alcohol abuse can reduce craving
Prayer	Trial showed no additional benefit when prayer added to standard treatment for alcohol abuse
Nutritional therapy	One trial shows gamma hydroxybutryic acid reduces withdrawal symptoms in alcohol abuse
Yoga	Comparison with dynamic group psychotherapy in methadone maintenance shows no advantage.

Professor Edzard Ernst's meta-analysis of the success rates of complementary therapies in treating addiction.

Defining addiction

Addiction	A behavioural and brain disorder marked by compulsive drug-seeking or other behaviour despite serious negative consequences
Substance dependence	Term used by World Health Organization and the American Psychiatric Association to describe drug addiction
Substance (drug) abuse/misuse	Use of a substance that, although hazardous, stops short of full-blown drug addiction
Alcoholism	Popular term for alcohol addiction
Alcohol dependence/harmful drinking	Medical terms for alcohol addiction
Alcohol abuse/misuse	Use of alcohol that is excessive but stops short of being full-blown alcohol dependence
Dependence	A state that develops as a result of brain adaptation produced by frequent drug use and marked by tolerance and withdrawal
Tolerance	Reduction in response to a drug after frequent use
Sensitization or reverse tolerance	Increase in response to a drug on frequent use
Withdrawal	Signs and symptoms that develop if a drug is stopped suddenly; produced by the brain being "out of balance"
Craving	Strong urge or desire to experience the reward effect of an addictive drug or behaviour
Lapse or slip	Isolated incident of drug-seeking behaviour/drug use after a period of abstinence
Relapse	Resumption of drug-seeking behaviour and drug use after a period of abstinence

General glossary

Agonist – a substance which binds at a receptor and activates it.

Antagonist – a substance which blocks a receptor so it cannot be activated.

ATP – adenosine triphosphate, the biochemical fuel of cells.

CREB – cyclic AMP response element-binding protein – name for a protein which turns on genes that can damp down the pleasure circuit in the brain; target of much research into addiction.

Dopamine – a neurotransmitter involved in producing feelings of pleasure/reward.

Endorphins – the brain's natural painkillers, similar in structure to the opiates and binding to the same receptors.

Enzyme – a protein that acts as a biological catalyst, helping break down various substances in the body

Excitatory neurotransmitter – a neurotransmitter that excites a receiving cell and encourages it to fire.

Frontal cortex – the outer layer of tissue at the front of the brain, linked with conscious thought and planning

Gamma-amino butyric acid (GABA) – inhibitory neurotransmitter involved in the action of alcohol and benzo-diazepine tranquillisers in the brain.

Gene – a piece of chemical code (DNA) which directs the production of proteins, mainly enzymes, in cells.

Inhibitory neurotransmitter – a neurotransmitter which inhibits a neuron from firing when it locks on to it.

Neuropeptide – a type of small protein found in the brain and nervous system.

Neurotransmitter – Chemicals produced by neurons in the brain which carry messages from one synapse to another.

Noradrenaline – neuro-transmitter with many functions including mood regulation and stress.

Nucleus accumbens – part of the brain involved in the reward circuit.

Opioid receptors – receptors which bind to opiates and endorphins.

P300 – wave of neural activity which sweeps from the back areas of the brain towards the front preceding voluntary actions and is detectable on an electroencephalogram (EEG) in brain monitoring experiments.

Receptor – a protein on the surface of a neuron (or other cell) which binds to a neurotransmitter (or other molecule), triggering a biochemical response in the cell.

Serotonin – a neurotransmitter with many functions, including mood regulation.

Synapse – the gap between two neurons, including the areas where neurotransmitters are released (pre-synaptic neuron) and received by receptors (post-synaptic neuron); essential link in transmitting information in the brain.

VTA – Ventral tegmental area – part of the brain involved in reward circuit.

Further Reading

Braun, S., Buzz: *The Science and Lore of Alcohol and Caffeine*, Oxford University Press Inc. USA, 1996.

Denning, P., Little, J., Glickman, A., *Over The Influence: The Harm Reduction Guide for Managing Drugs and Alcohol*, Guilford Press, 2004.

Drugscope, *Druglink Guide to Drugs*, 2004.

Earleywine, M., *Understanding Marijuana: A New Look at the Scientific Evidence*, Oxford University Press, 2002.

Edwards, G., *Alcohol: The Ambiguous Molecule*, Penguin, 2000.

Frances, R.J., Miller, S.I., (eds), *Clinical Textbook of Addictive Disorders*, 2nd Edition, The Guildford Press, 1998.

Ghodse, H., *Drugs and Addictive Behaviour: A Guide to Treatment*, 3rd Edition, Cambridge University Press, 2002.

Goldstein, A., *Addiction: From Biology to Drug Policy*, 2nd Edition, Oxford University Press, 2001.

Gossop, M., *Drug Addiction and Its Treatment*, Oxford University Press, 2003.

Gossop, M., *Living with Drugs*, 5th Edition, Ashgate, 2000.

Healy, D., *The Antidepressant Era*, Harvard University Press, 1997.

Johnstone, N., *A Head Full of Blue*, Bloomsbury, 2003.

McCance-Katz, E.F., Westley Clark, H., (eds), *Psychosocial Treatments; Key Readings in Addiction Psychiatry Series*, Brunner-Routledge, 2004.

O'Brien, C.P., "Drug Addiction and Drug Abuse", *Goodman and Gilman's The Pharmacological Basis of Therapeutics*, 10th Edition, Goodman Gilman (ed), McGraw-Hill, 2001.

Petersen, T., McBride, A. (eds), *Working With Substance Misusers*, Routledge, London, 2002.

Rudgley, R., *The Alchemy of Culture: Intoxicants in Society*, British Museum Press, 1993.

Rudgley, R., *The Encyclopedia of Psychoactive Substances*, Abacus, 1999.

Rusche, S., Friedman, D.P., *False Messengers: How Addictive Drugs Change the Brain*, Harwood, 1999.

Snyder, S., *Drugs and the Brain, Scientific American Books*, 1986.

Streetwise, Drugwise, Roman, E., James, R., Management Books, 2000, 1998.

Thombs, D.,L., *Introduction to Addictive Behaviors*, 2nd Edition, The Guilford Press, 1999.

Walton, J. (ed), *The Faber Book of Smoking*, Faber, 2000.

World Health Organisation, *Neuroscience of Psychoactive Substance Use and Dependence*, WHO, 2003.

Young, K., *Caught in the Net: How to recognize the Signs of Internet Addiction - a Sure-Fire Strategy for Recovery*, John Wiley, 1998.

Useful websites

www.ash.org.uk
Action on Smoking and Health

www.aa.org
Alcoholics Anonymous

www.ias.org
Institute of Alcohol Studies

www.na.org
Narcotics Anonymous

www.netaddiction.com
Centre for Online and Internet addiction

www.ca.org
Cocaine Anonymous

www.al-anon-alateen.org

www.gamblersanonymous.co.uk

Notes to the Text

Part One

[1] Goldstein, A., *Addiction: From Biology to Drug Policy*, Freeman, 2001, 86–87.

[2] ref. 1, ch. 7.

[3] Anthony, J.C. et al, "Comparative epidemiology of dependence on tobacco, alcohol, controlled substances and the inhalants: basic findings from the national comorbidity survey", *Experimental and Clinical Psychopharmacology*, 1994, 2, 244–268.

[4] ref. 1, p. 93.

[5] Higuchi, S. et al, "Alcohol and aldehyde dehydrogenase genotypes and drinking behavior in Japanese", *Alcohol Clinical and Experimental Research*, 1996, 20, 493–497.

[6] Pandey, S.C. et al., "Partial deletion of the cAMP response element-binding protein gene promotes alcohol drinking behavior", *Journal of Neuroscience*, 2004, 24, 5022–5030.

[7] Fowler, J.S. et al, "Cocaine: PET studies of cocaine pharmacokinetics, dopamine transporter availability and dopamine transporter occupancy", *Nuclear Medicine and Biology*, 2001, 28, 561–572.

[8] Agartz, I. et al, "MR volumetry during acute alcohol withdrawal and abstinence: a descriptive study", *Alcohol and Alcoholism*, 2003, 38, 71–8.

[9] www.stats.org/issuerecord.jsp?issue =true&ID=8 a discussion of myths about addiction

[10] Cloninger, C.R., Begleiter, H., (eds), "Genetics and biology of Alcoholism", *Banbury Report 33*, 1990, Cold Spring Harbor Laboratory Press.

[11] Stimson, G., Oppenheimer, E., *Heroin Addiction: Treatment and Control in Britain*, 1982, 229–252, Tavistock, London.

[12] World Health Organisation, *Neuroscience of Psychoactive Substance Use and Dependence*, WHO, 2004, ch. 2.

[13] ref.1, p. 44.

[14] Di Chiara, G., Imperato, A., "Drugs abused by humans preferentially increase synaptic dopamine concentrations in the mesolimbic system of freely moving rats", Proceedings of the National Academy of Sciences, 1988, 85, 5274–5278.

[15] Wise, R. A., Rompre, P. P., "Brain Dopamine and Reward", *Annual Reviews of Psychology*, 1989, 40, 191–225.

[16] Wise, R.A., "Drug Activation of Brain Reward Pathways", *Drug and Alcohol Dependence*, 1998, 51, 13–22.

[17] Cami, J., Farré, M., "Mechanisms of Disease: Drug Addiction", *New England Journal of Medicine*, 2003 349, 975–986.

[18] Verheul, R. et al., "A Threeway Psychobiological Model of Craving For Alcohol", *Alcohol and Alcoholism*, 1999, 77–82.

[19] ref. 12, p. 70

[20] Nutt, D., "Alcohol and the brain. Pharmacological insights for psychiatrists", *British Journal of Psychiatry*, 1999, 175, 114–119.

[21] Ballenger, J.C. et al, "Alcohol and central serotonin metabolism in man", *Archives of General Psychiatry*, 1979, 43, 446–457.

[22] Hesselbrock, V., et al, "P300 event-related potential amplitude as an endophenotype of alcoholism – evidence from the collaborative study on the genetics of alcoholism", *Journal of Biomedical Science*, 2001, 8, 77–82.

[23] Rehm, J. et al, "Alcohol as a risk factor for burden of disease", WHO, 2002.

[24] Ewing, J.A., "Detecting Alcoholism. The CAGE Questionnaire", *Journal of the American Medical Association*, 1984, 252, 1905–1907.

[25] Anthony, J.C., Warner, L.A.., Kessler, K.C., "Comparative epidemiology of dependence on tobacco, alcohol, controlled substances and the inhalants: basic findings from the national comorbidity survey", *Experimental Clinical Psychopharmacology*, 1994, 2, 244–268.

[26] Pianezza, M.I., et al, "Nicotine metabolism defect reduces smoking", *Nature*, 1998, 393, 750.

[27] Doll, R. et al, "Mortality in relation to smoking: 50 years' observations on male British doctors", *British Medical Journal*, 2004, 328, 1519–1535.

[28] Paterson, Nordberg, A., "Neuronal nicotinic receptors in the human brain", *Progress in Neurobiology*, 2000, 61, 75–111.

[29] Dani, J.A., De Biasa, M., "Cellular mechanisms of nicotine addiction Pharmacology", *Biochemistry and Behavior*, 2001, 70, 439–446.

[30] Di Chiara, G., Imperato, A., "Drugs abused by humans preferentially increase synaptic dopamine concentrations in the mesolimbic system of freely moving rats", Proceedings of the National Academy of Sciences, 1988, 85, 5274–8.

[31] ref.12.

[32] Tuomisto.,T., Hetherington, M.M. et al, "Psychological and physiological characteristics of sweet food addiction", International Journal of Eating Disorders, 1999, 25, 169–175.

[33] Pelchat, M.L., "Food cravings in young and elderly adults", Appetite, 1997, 28, 103–13.

[34] Pelchat, M.L., "Of human bondage: Food craving, obsession, compulsion and addiction", Physiology and Behavior, 2002, 76, 347–352.

[35] Gosnell, B.A., "Sucrose intake predicts rate of acquisition of cocaine self-administration", Psychopharmacology, 2000, 149, 286–292.

[36] McGee, H., "On Food and Cooking: The Science and Lore of the Kitchen", Harper Collins, 1984, ch. 8.

[37] Mercer, M.E., Holder, M.D., "Food cravings, endogenous opioid peptides and food intake", Appetite, 1997, 29, 325–352.

[38] Will, M.J., Franzblau, E.B. et al, "Nucleus Accumbens μ-opioids regulate intake of a high-fat diet via activation of a distributed brain network", Journal of Neuroscience, 2003, 23, 2882.

[39] Colantuoni, C., Rada, P. et al, "Evidence that intermittent excessive sugar intake causes endogenous opioid dependence", Obesity Research, 2002, 10, 478–488.

[40] Wurtman, R.J., Wurtman, J.J., "Brain serotonin, carbohydrate-craving, obesity and depression", Obesity Review, 1995, 3, 477.

[41] http://www.addictiontoday.co.uk/page.asp.

[42] http://www.addictions.co.uk/addiction.asp?id=exercise.

[43] http://www.theway.uk.com/ types/work.htm

[44] http://www.addictions.co.uk/addiction.asp?ID=sex

[45] http://www.netaddiction.com

[46] http://www.addictions.co.uk/statistics.asp

[47] http://www.addictions.co.uk/statistics.asp

[48] http://news.bbc.co.uk/1/hi/uk/3165546.stm

[49] http://www.spiritofrecovery.com/risk.html

[50] http://www.addictions.co.uk/weblink.asp?Link=http://www.codependents.org/

[51] http://www.m-a-h.net/library/selfinjury/article-si-facts.htm – explains the basics of self-injury.

Part Two

[52] Rawson, R.A. et al, "Addiction Pharmacotherapy 2000: New Options, New Challenges", Journal of Psychoactive Drugs, 2000, 32, 371–378.

[53] Aghajanian, C., "Tolerance of locus coeruleus neurons to morphine and suppression of withdrawal responses by clonidine", Nature, 1978, 276, 186–188.

[54] Kreek, M.J., "Methadone-related opioid agonist pharmacotherapy for heroin addiction. History, recent molecular and neurochemical research and future in mainstream medicine", Annals of the New York Academy of Sciences, 2000, 909, 186–216.

[55] Strang, J. et al, "Lofexidine for opiate detoxification: review of recent randomized and open trials", American Journal of Addictions, 1999, 8, 337–348.

[56] ref. 55.

[57] Strang, J. et al, "Opiate detoxification under anaesthesia", British Medical Journal, 1997, 315, 1249–1250; Brewer, C., "Opiate detoxification under anaesthesia", British Medical Journal, 1998, 316, 1983.

[58] Kaye, A.D., et al "Ultrarapid opiate detoxification: a review", Canadian Journal of Anaesthesia, 2003, 50, 663–671.

[59] ref. 54.

[60] Gossop, M. et al, "Patterns of improvement after methadone treatment: one year follow-up results from the National Treatment Outcome Study", Drug and Alcohol Dependence, 2000, 60, 275–286.

[61] Marsch, L.A., "The efficacy of methadone maintenance interventions in reducing illicit opiate use, HIV risk behaviour and criminality: a meta-analysis", *Addiction*, 1998, 93, 515-532.

[62] McLellan, A.T. et al, "The effects of psychosocial services in substance abuse treatment", *Journal of the American Medical Association*, 1993, 269, 1953-1959.

[63] Stimson, G., Oppenheimer, E. "Heroin Addiction. Treatment and control in Britain", 1982, p 229-252, Tavistock, London.

[64] Johnson, R. et al, "A comparison of levomethadyl acetate, buprenorphine and methadone for opioid dependence", *New England Journal of Medicine*, 2000, 343, 1290-1297.

[65] Kakko, J. et al, "One year retention and social function after buprenorphine-assisted relapse prevention treatment for heroin dependence in Sweden: a randomized, placebo-controlled trial", *The Lancet*, 2003, 361, 662-668.

[66] Glassman, A.H. et al, "Smoking, smoking cessation and major depression", *Journal of the American Medical Association*, 1990, 264, 1546-1549.

[67] ref 12, pp. 181-182.

[68] Kessler, R.C. et al "Lifetime and 12-month prevalence of DSM-III-R psychiatric disorders in the United States: Results from the National Comorbidity Survey", *Archives of General Psychiatry*, 1994, 51, 8-19

[69] ref. 12, p. 182–3.

[70] Johnson, R. et al, ref. 12, p. 183.

[71] ref. 12, p. 183.

[72] Nestler, E.J. et al, "Neurobiology of Depression", *Neuron*, 2002, 43, 13-25

[72 a] Froelich, J.C., "Opioid involvement in alcohol drinking", *Annals of the New York Academy of Sciences*, 1994, 739, 156–167.

[73] Streeton, C., Whelan, G., "Naltrexone, a relapse prevention maintenance treatment of alcohol dependence: a meta-analysis of randomized controlled trials", *Alcohol and Alcoholism*, 2001, 36, 544–552.

[73a] Kiefer, F. et al, "Comparing and Combining Naltrexone and Acamprosate in Relapse Prevention of Alcoholism: A Double-blind, Placebo-Controlled Study", *Archives of General Psychiatry*, 60, 92–99.

[74] Mason, B.J., "Treatment of alcohol-dependent outpatients with acamprosate: a clinical review", *Journal of Clinical Psychiatry*, 2001, 62 Suppl 20, 42–48.

[75] Graham, R. et al "New pharmacotherapies for alcohol dependence", *Medical Journal of Australia*, 2002, 177, 103-107.

[76] Kiefer, F. et al, "Comparing and Combining Naltrexone and Acamprosate in Relapse Prevention of Alcoholism: A Double-blind, Placebo-Controlled Study", *Archives of General Psychiatry*, 60, 92-99.

[77] National Institute for Clinical Excellence Technical Appraisal Guidance, 29, 2002.

[78] Solomon, L.J. et al, "Free nicotine patches plus proactive telephone peer support to help low-income women stop smoking", *Preventive Medicine*, 2000, 31, 68-72.

[79] Association of the British Pharmaceutical Industry, ABPI Data Sheet Compendium, 2000.

[80] Holmes, S. et al, "Bupropion as an aid to smoking cessation: a review of real-life effectivness", *International Journal of Clinical Practice* 2004 58 285-291.

[81] Jorendby, D.E. et al, "A controlled trial of sustained-release bupropion, a nicotine patch or both for smoking cessation", *New England Journal of Medicine*, 1999, 340, 685-691.

[82] Medicines Control Agency, Zyban (bupropion HCl SR) safety update, 8th April 2002.

[83] Roddy, E., "ABC of Smoking Cessation, Bupropion and other non-nicotine pharmacotherapies", *British Medical Journal*, 2004, 328, 509-511.

[84] Lancaster, T., Stead, L.F., "Mecamylamine (a nicotine antagonist) for smoking cessation (Cochrane Review)", *The Cochrane Library*, 2004, w,

[85] Moner, S.E., "Acupuncture and addiction treatment", *Journal of Addictive Diseases*, 1996, 15, 79-100.

[86] White, A.R. et al, "Acupuncture for smoking cessation (Cochrane Review)" *The Cochrane Library*, 2004, 2.

[87] Teitelbaum, S. et al, "Treatments for Compulsive Gambling" *Psych Central,* 2001, http://psychcentral.com/library/gambling_tx.htm

[88] Kim, S.W. et al, "Double-blind naltrexone and placebo comparison study in the treatment of pathological gambling", *Biological Psychiatry*, 2001 49 914-921.

[89] Pallanti, S., et al, "Nefazodone treatment of pathological gambling: a prospective open-label controlled trial", *Journal of Clinical Psychiatry*, 2002, 63 1034-1039

[90] Koran, L., "Chuong HW et al, Citalopram for compulsive shopping

disorder: an open-label study followed by double-blind discontinuation", *Journal of Clinical Psychiatry,* 2003, 64, 793–798.

[91] Gossop, M., et al, "Lapse, relapse and survival among opiate addicts after treatment: a prospective follow-up study", *British Journal of Psychiatry*, 1989, 154, 348–353.

[92] Gossop, M. et al, "Factors associated with abstinence, lapse or relapse to heroin use after residential treatmentl; protective effect of coping responses", *Addiction*, 2002, 97, 1259–1267.

[93] Bradley, B., et al, "Attributions and relapse in opiate addicts", *Journal of Consulting and Clinical Psychology*, 1992, 60, 470–472.

[94] Irvin, J. et al, "Efficacy of relapse prevention: a meta-analytic review", *Journal of Consulting and Clinical Psychology*, 1999, 67, 563–570.

[95] McCance-Katz, E.F., Westley Clark, H., (eds), "Relapse Prevention: An overview of Marlatt's cognitive-behavioural model", *Psychosocial Treatments; Key Readings in Addiction Psychiatry*, Brunner-Routledge, 2004.

[96] Chappell, J.N., DuPont, R.L., "Twelve step and mutual help programs for addictive disorders", *The Psychiatric Clinics of North America*, 1999, 22, 425–446.

[97] *Financial Times*, 15th June 2004

[98] Rocio, M. et al, "Treating cocaine addiction with viruses", Proceedings of the National Academy of Sciences, online, June 24, 2004.

[99] Advisory Council on the Misuse of Drugs, AIDS and Drug Misuse, Part 1 1988, HMSO.

[100] Advisory Council on the Misuse of Drugs, AIDS and Drug Misuse Update, 1993, HMSO.

[101] Stimson, G., "Has the United Kingdom averted a major epidemic or HIV-1 infection among drug injectors?", *Addiction,* 1996, 91, 1085–1088.

[102] Liese, B., Najavits, L., "Cognitive and behavioural therapies", *Substance Abuse: A Comprehensive Textbook*, ed Lowinson J et al., 1997, Williams and Wilkins.

[103] Project MATCH Research Group, "Matching alcoholism treatment to clinical heterogeneity. Project MATCH three-year drinking outcomes", *Alcoholism: Clinical and Experimental Research*, 1998, 22, 1300–1311.

[104] Anton, R.F. et al, "Naltrexone and cognitive behavioural therapy for the treatment of outpatient alcoholics: results of a placebo-controlled trial", *American Journal of Psychiatry*, 1999, 156, 1758–1764.

[105] Noonan, W.C., Moyers, T.B., "Motivational Interviewing in Psychosocial Treatments", *Key Readings in Addiction Psychiatry*, McCance-Katz, E.F., Westley Clark, H., Brunner-Routledge, 2004.

[106] Dunn, C. et al, "The use of brief interventions adapted from motivational interviewing across behavioural domains: a systematic review", *Addiction*, 2001, 1725–1742.

[107] Heather, N., "Effectiveness of brief interventions proved beyond reasonable doubt", *Addiction*, 2002, 97, 293–294.

[108] Wallace, P. et al, "Randomized control trial of general practitioner intervention in patients with excessive alcohol consumption", *British Medical Journal*, 1988, 297, 663–668.

[109] Biernacki P., *Pathways from Heroin Addiction: Recovery Without Treatment*, 1986, Temple University Press, Philadelphia.

[110] Westermeyer, J., et al, "Self-help strategies among patients with substance use disorder in Psychosocial Treatments", *Key Readings in Addiction Psychiatry*, McCance-Katz, E.F., Westley Clark, H., Brunner-Routledge, 2004.

[111] Glasser, W., *Positive Addiction*, HarperPerennial, 1985.

[112] White, A., Ernst, E., "Complementary or alternative medicine for substance misuse", *Working with Substance Misusers: A Guide to Theory and Practice,* ed. Petersen, T., McBride, A. (eds), 206–212.

Acknowledgements

Every care has been taken to contact copyright holders. However we apologize for any omissions and we shall, if informed, make corrections where necessary in any future editions. The publisher would like to thank the following for permission to reproduce their material:

Guilford Press for 'Cognitive Model of Drug Abuse' diagram from *Cognitive Therapy of Drug Abuse*, A.T. Beck, 1993 (page.151).

Alcoholics Anonymous for the 12 steps (page 141) and the case history of 'Sylvia' (page 111).

Penguin Group Ltd. for 'Arsenal v Liverpool' (page 95) reproduced from *Fever Pitch*, Nick Hornby, 1992.

Kimberly Young, Center for OnLine Addiction for the quiz on Internet addiction (pages 72–73).

Management Books 2000 for extracts from *Streetwise, Drugwise* (pages 17, 79, 83, 105, 137).

Action for Smoking on Health (ASH) for material previously published in STOP magazine (pages 53, 55. 91, 123, 124–125).

World Health Organisation for ICD-10 criteria for substance dependence (page 77).

Picture credits

Page 143: LAGUNA DESIGN/SCIENCE PHOTO LIBRARY

Page 103: KAIROS, LATIN STOCK/SCIENCE PHOTO LIBRARY

Page 39: PASCAL GOETGHELUCK/SCIENCE PHOTO LIBRARY

Page 44: LEONARD LESSIN, PETER ARNOLD INC./SCIENCE PHOTO LIBRARY

Page 127: ANNABELLA BLUESKY/ACUMEDIC/SCIENCE PHOTO LIBRARY

Page 31: DON FAWCETT/SCIENCE PHOTO LIBRARY

Page 47 Matt Windsor.

Author's acknowledgements

I would like to thank Dr Ken Checinski of St George's Hospital Medical School for advice and comments on the text and the staff at the Drugscope library for help and information.

Index